Learnikx's
Guide to
Opportunity Test
General Ability

Sibashis Nanda B.E.

IBM Certified Database Administrator
Project+ Certified Professional
Founder & CEO, Learnikx Education

A MindProBooks Initiative
www.mindprobooks.com

Learnikx's Guide to Opportunity Test General Ability
Sibashis Nanda

First Printing August 2020

ISBN **978-0-6488357-7-6**

Trademarks
All terms mentioned in this book that are known to be trademarks or service marks have been appropriately capitalized. Mindprobooks.com cannot attest to the accuracy of this information. Use of a term in this book should not be regarded as affecting the validity of any trademark or servicemark.

Warning and Disclaimer
Every effort has been made to make this book as complete and as accurate as possible, but no warranty or fitness is implied. The information provided is on an "as is" basis. The authors and the publisher shall have neither liability nor responsibility to any person or entity with respect to any loss or damages arising from the information contained in this book or from the use of the electronic material accompanying it.

We Want to Hear from You!

Welcome to the first print of *Learnikx's Guide to Opportunity Test General Ability*. As the reader of this book, you are our most important critic and commentator. We value your opinion and want to know what we're doing right, what we could do better, what areas you'd like to see us publish in, and any other words of wisdom you're willing to pass our way. You can email and let us know what you did or didn't like about this book, as well as what we can do to make our books better.

Please note that we cannot help you with technical problems related to the topic of this book, and we might not be able to reply to every message.

When you write, please be sure to include this book's title and author as well as your name and contact information.

Email: customerservice@mindprobooks.com

This page is intentionally left blank.

Odd One Out

Introduction

It is an activity of finding the differences in features between three or more words, things or living entities.

Type I – Word Classification

Classification means to observe the differences and similarities among various items such as things, letters, words, numbers from a group on the basis of their general property.

In classification items are grouped together on the basis of similarity and the odd one to be picked out, which does not belong to the group.

EXAMPLE 1

(a) Peacock
(b) Hen
(c) Eagle
(d) Penguin

Ans: (d)

Explanation: Penguins can't fly and Penguins can swim

EXAMPLE 2

(a) Bus
(b) Train
(c) Car
(d) Aeroplane

Ans: (d)

Explanation: Aeroplane can fly

EXAMPLE 3

(a) Hillary Clinton
(b) Barack Obama
(c) Abraham Lincoln
(d) Donald Trump

Ans: (a)

Explanation: Hillary Clinton has never been an US president till date.

EXAMPLE 4

(a) New York
(b) Washington
(c) Tokyo
(d) Chicago

Ans: (c)

Explanation: Tokyo is located in Japan.

EXAMPLE 5

(a) Carrot
(b) Tomato
(c) Beetroot
(d) Onion

Ans: (b)

Explanation: Tomatoes doesn't grow underground.

EXAMPLE 6

(a) 5
(b) 36
(c) 70
(d) 10

Ans: (b)

Explanation: 36 is not divisible by 5.

EXAMPLE 7

(a) Rose
(b) Lilly
(c) Cauliflower
(d) Jasmine

Ans: (c)

Explanation: Cauliflower is a vegetable.

EXAMPLE 8

(a) Hockey
(b) Football
(c) Cricket
(d) Chess

Ans: (d)

Explanation: Chess is an Indoor game; other games are outdoor games.

Type II – Number Classification

In number classification, there is a similarity among the numbers or group of numbers. The number classification is based on similarities like :

- Prime number
- Square and square roots of a number
- Cube and cube roots of a number
- Even and odd number
- Divisibility test of a number

EXAMPLE 9:

Find the odd one out.

(a) 72 – 43
(b) 68 – 40
(c) 85 – 57
(d) 55 – 27

Ans: (a)

Explanation: Except in the number pair 72 – 43, in all others the difference between the two number is 28.

68-40=28 ; 85-57=28; 55-27=28; 72-43=29. So 72-43 is odd one.

Type III – Alphabetical classification

In Alphabetical classification, there is similarity or pattern among the alphabets in the group. Students have to identify the pattern and select the one which does not follow the common pattern in the group. The relationship among alphabets may be as follows:

- Position of alphabets
- Vowel and constant
- Reverse order of alphabets
- Addition and Multiplication of position

EXAMPLE 10:

Find the odd one out.

(a) BCD
(b) QRS
(c) KMN
(d) WXY

Ans: (c)

Explanation: As B +1 = C, C +1 =D ; Q +1 = R; R +1= S ; W+1=X, X +1= Y, But K +2 = M, M+1 = N. So, KMN is odd one.

Exercise

Question 1: Find the Odd one out.

(a) Pond
(b) River
(c) Ocean
(d) Waterfall

Question 2: Find the Odd one out.

(a) Europe
(b) Africa
(c) Asia
(d) Canada

Question 3: Find the Odd one out.

(a) Flute
(b) Piano
(c) Violin
(d) Guitar

Question 4:Find the Odd one out.

(a) Yard
(b) Liter
(c) Meter
(d) Inch

Question 5: Find the Odd one out.

(a) Chameleon
(b) Crocodile
(c) Alligator
(d) Locust

Question 6:Find the Odd one out.

(a) Day: Night
(b) Up: Down
(c) Across: Along
(d) Small: Large

Question 7: Find the Odd one out.

(a) Mountain
(b) Hill
(c) Plateau
(d) Plane

Question 8: Find the Odd one out.

(a) Flag: Flagship
(b) Court: Courtship
(c) War: Worship
(d) Friend: Friendship

Question 9: Find the Odd one out.

(a) Father
(b) Mother
(c) Aunt
(d) Cousin

Question 10: Find the Odd one out.

(a) Triangle
(b) Rectangle
(c) Circle
(d) Square

Question 11: Find the Odd one out.

(a) Advise
(b) Counsel
(c) Suggest
(d) Direct

Question 12: Find the Odd one out.

(a) Pen
(b) Paper
(c) High lighter
(d) Marker

Question 13: Find the Odd one out.

(a) Cheetah
(b) Lion
(c) Bear
(d) Tiger

Question 14: Find the Odd one out.

(a) Hen
(b) Snake
(c) Swan
(d) Crocodile

Question 15: Find the Odd one out.

(a) Car
(b) Scooter
(c) Helicopter
(d) Cycle

Question 16: Find the Odd one out.

(a) Sparrow
(b) Swan
(c) Parrot
(d) Eagle

Question 17: Find the Odd one out.

(a) Steel
(b) Mercury
(c) Copper
(d) Zinc

Question 18: Find the Odd one out.

(a) Biscuits
(b) Chocolate
(c) Cake
(d) Bread

Question 19: Find the Odd one out.

(a) Raid
(b) Attack
(c) Assault
(d) Defense

Question 20: Find the Odd one out.

(a) Violet
(b) Blue
(c) Green
(d) White

Question 21:Find the Odd one out.

(a) Owl
(b) Crow
(c) Sparrow
(d) Bat

Question 22: Find the Odd one out.

(a) Yellow
(b) Pink
(c) Orange
(d) Green

Question 23: Find the Odd one out.

(a) Petrol
(b) Diesel
(c) Kerosene
(d) LPG

Question 24: Find the Odd one out.

(a) Leukemia
(b) AIDS
(c) Health
(d) Cancer

Question 25: Find the Odd one out.

(a) Leaf
(b) Stem
(c) Branches
(d) Garden

Question 26: Find the Odd one out.

(a) Book
(b) Journal
(c) Article
(d) Newspaper

Question 27: Find the Odd one out.

(a) 2378
(b) 7562
(c) 6662
(d) 1155

Question 28: Find the Odd one out.

(a) 15
(b) 17
(c) 6
(d) 12

Question 29: Find the Odd one out.

(a) 2,3
(b) 20,21
(c) 9,10
(d) 24,25

Question 30: Find the Odd one out.

(a) QRS
(b) XYZ
(c) STU
(d) MLN

Question 31: Find the Odd one out.

(a) 50,24
(b) 36,49
(c) 64,81
(d) 16,25

Question 32: Find the Odd one out.

(a) 5,21
(b) 29,45
(c) 48,68
(d) 71,87

Question 33: Find the Odd one out.

(a) 37
(b) 49
(c) 132
(d) 154

Question 34: Find the Odd one out.

(a) 21
(b) 69
(c) 81
(d) 83

Question 35: Find the Odd one out.

(a) 28
(b) 45
(c) 72
(d) 81

Question 36: Find the Odd one out.

(a) 49
(b) 63
(c) 77
(d) 81

Question 37: Find the Odd one out.

(a) 140
(b) 240
(c) 360
(d) 480

Question 38:Find the Odd one out.

(a) RAT
(b) CAT
(c) SAT
(d) GET

Question 39:Find the Odd one out.

(a) OTP
(b) ABA
(c) SZX
(d) UVB

Question 40:Find the Odd one out.

(a) 144,81
(b) 169,600
(c) 196,121
(d) 100,225

Question 41:Find the Odd one out.

(a) 13
(b) 26
(c) 14
(d) 88

Question 42: Find the Odd one out.

(a) 286 682
(b) 397 793
(c) 475 547
(d) 369 963

Question 43: Find the Odd one out.

(a) 5,58
(b) 6,69
(c) 7,80
(d) 8,90

Answers

1. (d)	16. (b)	31. (a)
2. (d)	17. (b)	32. (c)
3. (a)	18. (b)	33. (a)
4. (b)	19. (d)	34. (c)
5. (d)	20. (d)	35. (a)
6. (c)	21. (d)	36. (d)
7. (d)	22. (b)	37. (a)
8. (c)	23. (d)	38. (d)
9. (d)	24. (c)	39. (b)
10. (c)	25. (d)	40. (b)
11. (d)	26. (c)	41. (a)
12. (b)	27. (d)	42. (c)
13. (c)	28. (b)	43. (d)
14. (a)	29. (a)	
15. (d)	30. (d)	

Hints and Solutions

1. Except waterfall, all other belongs to the same group.

2. Except Canada, all others are continent while Canada is one of the country in North American Continent.

3. Except Flute, all other are string based instruments.

4. Except Litre, all other are length units while Litre is a liquid unit.

5. Except Locust, all others are reptile, while Locust is a large Insect.

6. Day – Night, Up – Down and Small – Large word pairs denote the opposite relationship among them. But Across and Along are synonym.

7. Except Plane, all items have height.

8. War and Worship are not related words.

9. Except Cousin, all others belong to the same generation.

10. Except Circle, all other figures are made up of straight lines.

11. Except Direct, all others are synonyms.

12. Except paper, all other are used on paper.

13. Except Bear, all other belongs to Cat family.

14. Except Hen, all other can live in Water.

15. Except Cycle, all others run on fuel.

16. Only Swan is water bird among them.

17. Except Mercury, all others are solid.

18. All except chocolate are baked items.

19. All except defense are forms of attack.

20. All except white are colors of the rainbow.

21. Except Bat, all others are flying birds. 'Bat' is a flying mammal.

22. Except Pink, all others colors are seen in the rainbow.

23. Except LPG, all others are liquids while LPG is a Liquified Petroleum Gas.

24. Except health, all others are different kinds of disease.

25. Except Garden, all others are parts of a tree.

26. Except Article, all others are combination of various agenda while article is centralised on one agenda.

27. 2+3+7+8= 20; 7+5+6+2= 20; 6+6+6+2= 20; but 1+1+5+5= 12.

28. Except 17, all others are composite numbers.

29. Except 2,3 , all others numbers are divisible, while 2 & 3 are prime numbers.

30. Q +1= R, R+1 = S ; X+1= Y, Y+1=Z; S+1=T,T+1=U; M-1=L,L+2=N.

31. All the numbers are square root numbers except 50,24

32. 21 -5 = 16 ; 45 -29 = 16; 68-48 = 20; 87- 71= 16.So, 48,68 is the odd one.

33. 37 is the only prime number in the group.

34. 81 is the only perfect square number in the group.

35. Except 28,all the other numbers are divisible by 9.

36. Each of the number except 81, is divisible by 7.

37. Each of the number except 140, is a multiples of 120.

38. All the other groups end with AT, except ET.

39. There is no repetition of any letter in any other group, except ABA.

40. Except 169,600, all other both numbers are perfect square numbers.

41. Only 13 is a prime number.

42. All the numbers are perfectly reversed, except option (c).

43. Except 8-90, in all others one number is even and other number is odd while in 8-90, both numbers are even.

Coding and Decoding

Introduction:

Coding-Decoding is the process of transferring information from one to other secretly using Codes.

Coding is a Process of converting of readable data into non-readable form. So that only Sender and the receiver know it's meaning, but the others can't understand its meaning.

Decoding is reverse process. It's a process of converting a non-readable message to readable format.

Type I: BASIC CODING

In Basic Coding, Each alphabets given a value in a sequence.

Let say, A=1, B=2, C=3,D=4.......Y=25 and Z=26

Similarly it can also coded in descending order too.

Like, A=26, B=25, C=24, D=23.....Y=2 and Z=1

EXAMPLE 1

"One" can be coded as

(a) 15145
(b) 20231
(c) 00001
(d) 15143

Ans: (a)

Explanation: O=15, N=14, E=5. So the answer is 15145.

EXAMPLE 2

"JACK" can be coded as

(a) 1815195
(b) 101311
(c) 111311
(d) 101310

Ans: (b)

Explanation: J=10, A=1, C=3, K=11, So the answer is 101311.

Type II- NUMBER CODING

Introduction:

In number coding, the alphabets are assigned to a specific codes of numbers unlike the "Alphabet coding" model.

EXAMPLE 1

If TWO is coded as 547 and TEN Is coded as 512, then what will be coded for WON?

(a) 517
(b) 751
(c) 472
(d) 712

Ans: (c)

Explanation: In TWO, T=5,W=4,O=7. In TEN, T=5, E=1,N=2.

So, for WON, W=4, O=7, N=2. The answer is 472.

EXAMPLE 2

If TALK is coded as 9876 and COME is coded as1234, then how LOCK will be coded?

(a) 7216
(b) 8916
(c) 1397
(d) 6432

Ans: (a)

Explanation: T=9, A=8, L=7,K=6 and C=1,O=2,M=3,E=4

So, LOCK is L=7,O=2,C=1,K=6. The answer is 7216.

Type III- ALPHABET CODING

Introduction:

In Alphabet coding, each alphabet is coded as another alphabet using one or two logical patterns such as Addition or Subtraction.

EXAMPLE 1:

If YES is coded as ZFT, then how NO can be written in that Code?

(a) ON
(b) OP
(c) PO
(d) MN

Ans: (b)

Explanation: Word YES is coded as ZFT that is Z is next alphabet of Y, F is next alphabet of E, T is next alphabet of S. By following the sequence, The next Alphabet of N is O and of O is P. So The answer is OP.

EXAMPLE 2

If EYE is coded as HBH, then how EAR will be written?

(a) HAR
(b) GCT
(c) IEV
(d) HDU

Ans: (d)

Explanation: E=H, Y=B, E=H. It shows that 3rd letter of the alphabet is used for coding. By following that E=H, A=D, R=U. The answer is HDU.

Exercise

Question 1: If WATER is coded as XBUFS, then how PUBLIC will be written?

(a) RVAMJD
(b) QVCMJD
(c) QWDNJE
(d) QVCNJD

Question 2: If GAP is coded as FZO, then how PUBLISH will be written?

(a) OTAKHRG
(b) OSAKHRG
(c) QVCMJTI
(d) OTBKHRG

Question 3: If CIVIL is coded as EKXKN, then how GENERAL will be written?

(a) IGPGSCM
(b) FDMDQZK
(c) IGPGTCN
(d) DCLCPYJ

Question 4:If CABLE is coded as AYZJC, then how PATTERN will be written?

(a) NBSSFQM
(b) NYRRCPL
(c) NZPPDQL
(d) NYQQCPL

Question 5: If SCIENCE is coded as TBJDOBF, then how HISTORY will be written?

(a) IHTSPQZ

(b) IJRSPSX
(c) IHTSPRZ
(d) IHSTPRZ

Question 6: If VISION is coded as WKVMTT, then howEYE will be written?

(a) FAF
(b) FAH
(c) FZF
(d) DXD

Question 7:If NATURE is coded as ETARUN, then how DONKEY will be written?

(a) YONEKD
(b) YNOKED
(c) YEKNOD
(d) YNOEKD

Question 8: If MASTER is coded as RETSAM, then how CRICKET will be written?

(a) TEKCICR
(b) TEKCIRC
(c) TEKCICC
(d) TKECIRC

Question 9: If ENGLISH is coded as EHSILGN, then how POWER will be written?

(a) PWORE
(b) PREOW
(c) PREWO
(d) PERWO

Question 10: If ENGLAND is coded as EOIOESJ, then how FRANCE will be written?

(a) FSCQGJ
(b) FCSQGJ
(c) FCSGQJ
(d) FVQJCG

Question 11:If PEN is coded as NEQ, then how HOT will be written?

(a) TOH
(b) TOJ
(c) TOI
(d) TOY

Question 12: If SILVER is coded as THMUFQ, then how GOLD will be written?

(a) HNMC
(b) HMNC
(c) HPME
(d) HCMN

Question 13: If MONKEY is coded as OMKNYE, then how CONVEX will be written?

(a) XEVNOC
(b) OCVNXE
(c) OCNVXE
(d) ODVMXD

Question 14: If WORLD is coded as YQTNF, then how CONCAVE will be written?

(a) EQPECXG
(b) EQPDCXH

(c) EQQECXY
(d) EQPECXJ

Question 15: If MULTIPLE is coded as TLUMELPI, then how MUSHROOM will be written?

(a) MOOHHSUM
(b) HSUMMOOR
(c) HSUMROOM
(d) HSMUMOOR

Question 16: If EARTHQUAKE is coded as HEARTEQUAK, then how PUBLISHING will be written?

(a) TEARHGUBLS
(b) IPUBLGSHIN
(c) IGPUBLSHIN
(d) IPUBLGSHIM

Question 17: If AUGUST is coded as YWEWQV, then how JUICER will be written?

(a) HVJDFS
(b) KVJDDQ
(c) HWGEDT
(d) HWGECT

Question 18:If HOUSE is written as LSYWI, then how SUPER will be written?

(a) WYTIV
(b) WZTIW
(c) WYTIU
(d) WYITV

Question 19: If EXAM is coded as XMXM, then how BOMBAY will be written?

(a) OBAYOBAY
(b) OBYOBY
(c) OBYBOM
(d) YBOYBO

Question 20:If SYDNEY is coded as PVAKBV, then how LONDON will be written?

(a) ILKALK
(b) IMKAMK
(c) HMKAMK
(d) IIKALK

Question 21:If HAND is coded as HCRJ, then how LEG will be written?

(a) KGL
(b) LKG
(c) LGK
(d) KLG

Question 22: If A=1, B=2, C=3 and so on, then FOOD can be coded as?

(a) 615154
(b) 515152
(c) 415151
(d) 615152

Question 23:If ASIA is coded as VNDV, then how CHINA will be written?

(a) VIDCX
(b) XCDIV

(c) YDEJW
(d) XCDJV

Question 24:If A=1, B=2, C=3 and so on, then HAPPY can be coded as?

(a) 81161622
(b) 81161623
(c) 81161625
(d) 81161622

Question 25:If HYDEN is coded as GWAAI, then how SMITH will be written?

(a) RKFQC
(b) RKFPC
(c) RKGQC
(d) RKFQD

Question 26:If STRAIT is coded as SIARTT, then how MIRROR will be written?

(a) MOIRRR
(b) RORRIM
(c) MORRIR
(d) MORRRI

Question 27: If MACHINE is coded as CAMHENI, then how CONSULT will be written?

(a) NOCSTLU
(b) NOCTLUS
(c) NOCSULT
(d) LUSTNOC

Question 28: If A=1, B=2, C=3 and so on, then GOLD can be coded as?

(a) 715123
(b) 711224
(c) 715124
(d) 711111

Question 29: If A=1, B=2, C=3 and so on, then SILVER can be coded as?

(a) 1991222518
(b) 1991222320
(c) 1991222410
(d) 1991222110

Question 30: If WELCOME is coded as EMOCLEW, then how DANGER will be written?

(a) REGDNA
(b) REGNAD
(c) REGNDA
(d) REGAND

Question 31:If A=2, B=2, C=3 and so on, then what will be the code for DEABH?

(a) 56332
(b) 56239
(c) 56318
(d) 56329

Question 32: If BGHAI is coded as 27819, then how FICDE will be written?

(a) 53246
(b) 69345

(c) 68336

(d) 68345

Question 33:If GATE is code as 5362 and PLAN is coded as 7938, then how PLATE will be written?

(a) 79362

(b) 79536

(c) 79368

(d) 79638

Question 34: If BOSE is coded as 6831 and PERMIT is coded as 714295, then how ORBIT will be written?

(a) 84376

(b) 84695

(c) 84723

(d) 84231

Question 35: If MOVIE is coded as 53721 and JUMP is coded as 6859, then how VUMPE will be written?

(a) 78591

(b) 76591

(c) 76253

(d) 87591

Question 36:If EDUCATION is coded as 548216397, then how CAUTION will be written?

(a) 2637645

(b) 2186397

(c) 8126397

(d) 1286397

Question 37: If 46325 is coded as 55416, then how 76284 will be written?

(a) 85175
(b) 85275
(c) 85375
(d) 84375

Question 38: If 5348 is coded as 4114, then how 2567 will be written?

(a) 1333
(b) 1345
(c) 2333
(d) 4357

Question 39: If SHARP is coded as 53824, then how RSPH will be written?

(a) 8345
(b) 3825
(c) 2543
(d) 2453

Question 40: If TRAIN is coded as 63845, the how ANT will be written?

(a) 856
(b) 865
(c) 658
(d) 385

Question 41: If MASTER is coded as 538421 and RABBIT is coded as 136674, then how the word TASTE will be written?

(a) 42842
(b) 43832

(c) 43842

(d) 43942

Question 42: If MASTER is coded as 538421 and RABBIT is coded as 136674, then how the word BITTER will be written?

(a) 674421

(b) 675512

(c) 673312

(d) 647721

Question 43: If MASTER is coded as 538421 and RABBIT is coded as 136674, then how the word EASTER will be written?

(a) 284213

(b) 248321

(c) 238421

(d) 237422

Question 44: If MASTER is coded as 538421 and RABBIT is coded as 136674, then how the word BARBER will be written?

(a) 631621

(b) 637622

(c) 638621

(d) 641622

Question 45: If MASTER is coded as 538421 and RABBIT is coded as 136674, then how the word TIBET will be written?

(a) 16724

(b) 47624

(c) 17624

(d) 17524

Question 46: If MASTER is coded as 538421 and RABBIT is coded as 136674, then how the word MARS will be written?

(a) 5138
(b) 5318
(c) 5183
(d) 5328

Question 47: If MASTER is coded as 538421 and RABBIT is coded as 136674, then how the word AIM will be written?

(a) 573
(b) 735
(c) 375
(d) 385

Question 48: If MASTER is coded as 538421 and RABBIT is coded as 136674, then how the word STAR will be written?

(a) 8314
(b) 8143
(c) 8134
(d) 8431

Question 49: If MASTER is coded as 538421 and RABBIT is coded as 136674, then how the word RETIRE will be written?

(a) 134812
(b) 134713
(c) 124712
(d) 128723

Question 50: If MASTER is coded as 538421 and RABBIT is coded as 136674, then how the word TERMITE will be written?

(a) 4315642
(b) 4215742

(c) 4235746

(d) 4215842

Question 51: If PRESIDENT is coded as 734281456 and STUDENT is coded as 2691456, then how DENTIST will be written?

(a) 1457826
(b) 1456826
(c) 1564826
(d) 1826456

Question 52: If PRESIDENT is coded as 734281456 and STUDENT is coded as 2691456, then how EDEN will be written?

(a) 4245
(b) 4415
(c) 4145
(d) 4541

Question 53: If PRESIDENT is coded as 734281456 and STUDENT is coded as 2691456, then how TENENT will be written?

(a) 654456
(b) 645465
(c) 645456
(d) 654656

Question 54: If PRESIDENT is coded as 734281456 and STUDENT is coded as 2691456, then how STREET will be written?

(a) 263446
(b) 236446
(c) 244636
(d) 236464

Question 55: If PRESIDENT is coded as 734281456 and STUDENT is coded as 2691456, then how DRESS will be written?

(a) 14332
(b) 12243
(c) 13224
(d) 13422

Question 56: If PRESIDENT is coded as 734281456 and STUDENT is coded as 2691456, then how PERSUED will be written?

(a) 7349241
(b) 7432941
(c) 7924143
(d) 7344921

Question 57: If PRESIDENT is coded as 734281456 and STUDENT is coded as 2691456, then how RENT will be written?

(a) 4356
(b) 6543
(c) 3546
(d) 3456

Question 58: If PRESIDENT is coded as 734281456 and STUDENT is coded as 2691456, then how PRESSURE will be written?

(a) 73422934
(b) 74322934
(c) 72234934
(d) 74393422

Question 59: If PRESIDENT is coded as 734281456 and STUDENT is coded as 2691456, then how NEST will be written?

(a) 5264
(b) 5426

(c) 5624

(d) 4526

Question 60: If PRESIDENT is coded as 734281456 and STUDENT is coded as 2691456, then how TISSUE will be written?

(a) 622894

(b) 682249

(c) 682294

(d) 682243

Answers

1. (b)	13. (b)	25. (b)	37. (c)	49. (c)
2. (a)	14. (a)	26. (c)	38. (a)	50. (b)
3. (c)	15. (b)	27. (a)	39. (c)	51. (b)
4. (b)	16. (b)	28. (c)	40. (a)	52. (c)
5. (a)	17. (d)	29. (a)	41. (c)	53. (c)
6. (b)	18. (a)	30. (b)	42. (a)	54. (a)
7. (d)	19. (b)	31. (b)	43. (c)	55. (d)
8. (b)	20. (a)	32. (b)	44. (a)	56. (b)
9. (c)	21. (c)	33. (a)	45. (b)	57. (d)
10. (a)	22. (a)	34. (b)	46. (b)	58. (a)
11. (c)	23. (b)	35. (a)	47. (c)	59. (b)
12. (a)	24. (c)	36. (b)	48. (d)	60. (c)

Hints and Solutions

1. P U B L I C $\boxed{+1}$
   ↓ ↓ ↓ ↓ ↓ ↓
   Q V C M J D

2. P U B L I S H $\boxed{-1}$
   ↓ ↓ ↓ ↓ ↓ ↓ ↓
   O T A K H R G

3. G E N E R A L $\boxed{+2}$
   ↓ ↓ ↓ ↓ ↓ ↓ ↓
   I G P G T C N

4. P A T T E R N $\boxed{-2}$
   ↓ ↓ ↓ ↓ ↓ ↓ ↓
   N Y R R C P L

5. H   I   S   T   O   R   Y
   ↓$\boxed{+1}$ ↓$\boxed{-1}$ ↓$\boxed{}$ ↓$\boxed{+1}$ ↓$\boxed{-1}$ ↓$\boxed{+1}$ ↓$\boxed{-1}$ +1
   I   H   T   S   P   Q   Z

6. E   Y   E
   ↓$\boxed{+1}$ ↓$\boxed{+2}$ ↓$\boxed{+3}$
   F   A   H

7. 1st and 6th letters, 2nd and 3rd letters, 4th and 5th letters are interchanged. So DONKEY is coded as YNOEKD.

8. CRICKET is written from back side.

9.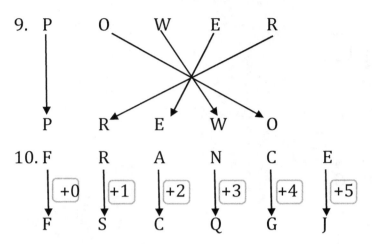

10.
F	R	A	N	C	E
+0	+1	+2	+3	+4	+5
F	S	C	Q	G	J

11. 1st letter forwarded by one letter and replaced in 3rd place, 3rd letter moved to 1st place, 2nd remained constant. So HOT is coded as TOI.

12.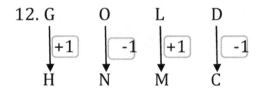
G	O	L	D
+1	-1	+1	-1
H	N	M	C

13. 1st and 2nd letters, 3rd and 4th letters, 5th and 6th letters are interchanged and coded as OCVNXE.

14.
C	O	N	C	A	V	E
						+2
E	Q	P	E	C	X	G

15.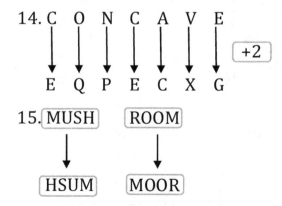

MUSH → HSUM

ROOM → MOOR

16.

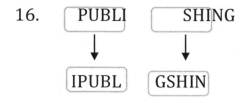

17. 1st , 3rd and 5th letters are moved backward by two letters, and 2nd, 4th and 6th letters are moved forward by two letters and so JIUCER is coded as HWGECT.

18.

```
S   U   P   E   R
|   |   |   |   |        +4
↓   ↓   ↓   ↓   ↓
W   Y   T   I   V
```

19. All the Even letters repeated. So BOMBAY is coded as OBYOBY.

20.

```
L   O   N   D   O   N
|   |   |   |   |   |        -3
↓   ↓   ↓   ↓   ↓   ↓
I   L   K   A   L   K
```

21.

```
L       E       G
|  +0   |  +2   |  +4
↓       ↓       ↓
L       G       K
```

22. If A=1, B=2, C=3 , Similarly F=6, O=15, O=15 and D=4 .

23.

```
C   H   I   N   A
|   |   |   |   |        -5
↓   ↓   ↓   ↓   ↓
X   C   D   I   V
```

24. If A=1, B=2, C=3 , Similarly H=8, A=1, P=16, P=16 and Y=25.

25.
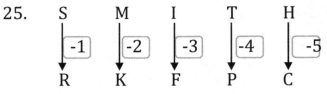

S	M	I	T	H
-1	-2	-3	-4	-5
R	K	F	P	C

26.
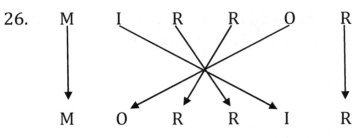

M I R R O R

M O R R I R

27.
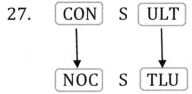

CON S ULT

NOC S TLU

28. If A=1, B=2, C=3 , Similarly G=7, O=15, L=12, D=4.

29. If A=1, B=2, C=3 , Similarly S=19, I=9, L=12, V=22, E=5, R=18.

30.   The words are written from backside.

31. If A=2, B=3, C=4, D=5, E=6, F=7, G=8, H=9. DEABH = 56239.

32. If A=1, B=2, C=3, D=4 and so on. Then FICDE = 69345.

33.   G A T E P L A N

       5 3 6 2 7 9 3 8 .

   As coded above PLATE = 79362

34.   B O S E P R M I T

       6 8 3 1 7 4 2 9 5

   As coded above ORBIT = 84695.

35. M O V I E J U P

5 3 7 2 1 6 8 9

As coded above VUMPE = 78592

36. E D U C A T I O N

5 4 8 2 1 6 3 9 7

As coded above CAUTION = 2186397

37.
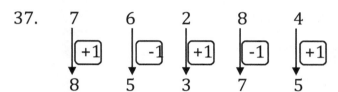

38.

2   5   6   7

-1   -2   -3   -4

1   3   3   3

39. S H A R P

5 3 8 2 4

As coded above RSPH = 2543

40. T R A I N

6 3 8 4 5

As coded above ANT = 856

41. M A S T E R B I

5 3 8 4 2 1 6 7

As coded above TASTE = 43842

42. As coded in Q.41 above BITTER = 674421

43. As coded in Q.41 above EASTER = 238421

44. As coded in Q.41 above BARBER = 631621

45. As coded in Q.41 above TIBET = 47624

46. As coded in Q.41 above MARS = 5318

47. As coded in Q.41 above AIM = 375

48. As coded in Q.41 above STAR = 8431

49. As coded in Q.41 above RETIRE = 124712

50. As coded in Q.41 above TERMITE = 4215742

51.　　P　R　E　S　I　D　E　N　T　U

　　　　7　3　4　2　8　1　4　5　6　9

As coded above DENTIST = 1456826

52. As coded in Q.51 above EDEN = 4145

53. As coded in Q.51 above TENENT = 645456

54. As coded in Q.51 above STREET = 263446

55. As coded in Q.51 above DRESS = 13422

56. As coded in Q.51 above PERSUED = 7432941

57. As coded in Q.51 above RENT = 3456

58. As coded in Q.51 above PRESSURE = 73422934

59. As coded in Q.51 above NEST = 5426

60. As coded in Q.51 above TISSUE = 682294.

Analogy

Introduction:

Analogy means Similarity or bearing Resemblance. Analogy is comparison between two things that are similar to two other things.

Type 1: WORD ANALOGY

Introduction:

In word analogy, have to find relationship between given words in a pair.

EXAMPLE 1:

Doctor is related to Hospital, Then Teacher is related to?

(a) School
(b) Industry
(c) Field
(d) Laboratory

Ans: (a)

Explanation: As Doctor works in Hospital. Similarly, Teacher works in School.

EXAMPLE 2:

Cow is related to Calf, Then Hen is related to?

(a) Duckling
(b) Kitten
(c) Chicken
(d) Cock

Ans: (c)

Explanation: Calf is the young one of Cow. Similarly, Chicken is the young one of Hen.

EXAMPLE 3:

Tiger is related to Tigress, Then Lion is related to?

(a) Lady
(b) Niece
(c) Mare
(d) Lioness

Ans: (d)

Explanation: Female tiger is called as Tigress. Similarly Female lion is called as Lioness.

Type II – NUMBER ANALOGY

In number analogy, Numbers are given in pair and students has to find the relationship among the numbers.

EXAMPLE 1

'26' is related as '12'. In the same way 35 is related to?

(a) 27
(b) 31
(c) 15
(d) 25

Ans: (c)

Explanation: 26 is related as 2 x 6 = 12. Similarly 35 is related as 3 x 5 = 15.

EXAMPLE 2:

'17' is related as '8'. In the same way '25' is related to?

(a) 10
(b) 7
(c) 16
(d) 6

Ans: (b)

Explanation: 17 is related as 1+7 = 8. Similarly 25 is related as 2+5 = 7.

EXAMPLE 3:

'58' is related as '69'. In the same way '25' is related to?

(a) 70
(b) 26
(c) 36
(d) 35

Ans: (c)

Explanation: 58 + 11 = 69. Similarly, 25+11= 36.

EXAMPLE 4:

'42' is related as '2'. In the same way '93' is related to?

(a) 1
(b) 2
(c) 3
(d) 4

Ans: (c)

Explanation: 4÷2 = 2. Similarly 9÷3 = 3.

EXAMPLE 5:

'24' is related to 45. In the same way '48' is related to?

(a) 90
(b) 89
(c) 69
(d) 114

Ans: (b)

Explanation: (2 x 2)= 4 & (4+1)= 5. Similarly, (4 x 2) = 8 & (8+1)=9.

The answer is 89.

Type III – Figural Analogy

Analogy implies similarity and corresponding. If a pair of figures exhibits some kind of relationship on the basis of shape, size, rotation, interchange of elements, number of elements etc., and another pair of figures exhibits the same kind of relationship between them, then the two pairs are said to be analogous to each other.

In this type two pairs of figures are given which are related to each other in some ways. Students are required to find out the relationship between the two figures of the first pair and on the basis of similar relationship, we have to find out the second/missing figure of the second pair from amongst the answer figures, so that the similar relationship is established between the two figures.

1. SIZE OF FIGURES

In this type of questions, the size of the figures in the first figure of one pair are interchanged to obtain the second figure of the pair, *i.e.,* the smaller figure becomes larger and the larger figure becomes smaller. By the following the same pattern, the missing figure of another part is to be found out.

EXAMPLE 1:

Find the figure from the answer figure that will replace the question mark (?) from the problem figure.

Problem figures

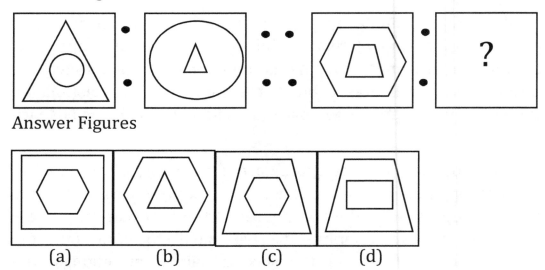

Answer Figures

    (a)   (b)   (c)   (d)

Ans: (c)

Explanation: By the careful analysis of first part of the problem figure, we find that from first to second figure, the large triangle becomes small and small circle becomes large. In the same manner, from third to fourth figure, the large hexagon become becomes small and the small trapezoid becomes large as shown in figure (c).

2. ROTATION OF FIGURES

In this types of questions, first figure of one pair rotates by a certain angle to obtain the second figure of that paid. By following the same rotation pattern, the missing figure of another pair is to be found.

EXAMPLE 2

Problem Figures

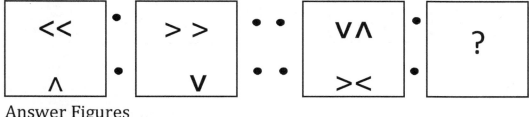

Answer Figures

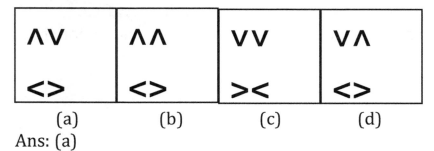

(a)   (b)   (c)   (d)

Ans: (a)

Explanation: The first group of figure, the above elements rotate 180° clockwise direction. Same as the third figure will seem as option (a) in answer figure.

3. NUMBER OF LINES/ ELEMENTS

In this type of questions, the number of lines get increased or decreased in the first figure of one pair to obtain the second figure of the pair. By following the same pattern, the missing figure of another pair is to be found out.

Problem figures

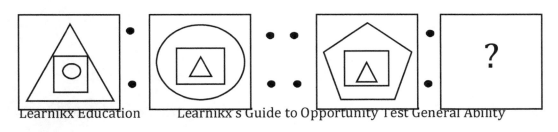

Answer Figures

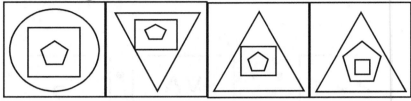

Ans: (c)

Explanation: In the first group the inner 'O' becomes outer 'O' and the outer △ becomes the inner△ in the new figure. Same as the third figure would be like figure (c) in the option in answer figure.

Exercise

Question 1: Select the related words from the given alternatives.

Vacation : Holiday :: Vocation : ?

(a) Money
(b) Pleasure
(c) Degree
(d) Career

Question 2: Select the related words from the given alternatives.

Waiter : Restaurant :: Lawyer : ?

(a) Laboratory
(b) Court
(c) Ship
(d) Theatre

Question 3: Select the related words from the given alternatives.

Sailor : Ship :: Artist : ?

(a) Field
(b) Theatre
(c) Pitch
(d) Office

Question 4: Select the related words from the given alternatives.

Engineer : Site :: Worker : ?

(a) Court
(b) Hospital
(c) Factory
(d) Cockpit

Question 5 : Select the related words from the given alternatives.

Farmer : Crop :: Goldsmith : ?

(a) Furniture
(b) Ornaments
(c) Clothes
(d) Newspaper

Question 6: Select the related words from the given alternatives.

Author : Books :: Editor : ?

(a) Shoes
(b) Designs
(c) Ballet
(d) Newspaper

Question 7: Select the related words from the given alternatives.

Chef : Food :: Choreographer : ?

(a) Crop
(b) Ballet
(c) Ornaments
(d) Clothes

Question 8: Select the related words from the given alternatives.

Carpenter : Furniture :: Tailor : ?

(a) Clothes
(b) Book
(c) Newspaper
(d) Design

Question 9: Select the related words from the given alternatives.

Cat : Kitten :: Lion : ?

(a) Pony
(b) Cub
(c) Puppy
(d) Chicken

Question 10: Select the related words from the given alternatives.

Dog : Puppy :: Butterfly : ?

(a) Caterpillar
(b) Lamb
(c) Duckling
(d) Kitten

Question 11: Select the related words from the given alternatives.

Wall : Brick :: Shoes : ?

(a) Fibre
(b) Wood
(c) Leather
(d) Grapes

Question 12:Select the related words from the given alternatives.

Cloth : Fiber :: Book : ?

(a) Paper
(b) Leather
(c) Yarn
(d) Seed

Question 13: Select the related words from the given alternatives.

Omelet : Egg :: Oil : ?

(a) Wood
(b) Seed
(c) Grapes
(d) Brick

Question 14:Select the related words from the given alternatives.

Furniture : Wood :: Butter : ?

(a) Egg
(b) Grapes
(c) Yarn
(d) Milk

Question 15: Select the related words from the given alternatives.

Play : Actor :: Concert : ?

(a) Musician
(b) Carpenter
(c) Architect
(d) Editor

Question 16:Select the related words from the given alternatives.
Right : Wrong :: Pleasure : ?

(a) Happy
(b) Joy
(c) Wonderful
(d) Sad

Question 17: Select the related words from the given alternatives.

Life : Death :: Beginning : ?

(a) Era
(b) End
(c) Time

(d) Commence

Question 18: Select the related word/letters/number from the given alternatives.

UHCDN : VIDEO :: OKZXDQ : ?

(a) REPLAY
(b) REPOSE
(c) PLAYER
(d) OPPOSE

Question 19: Select the related word/letters/number from the given alternatives.

64: 8 :: 289 : ?

(a) 17
(b) 27
(c) 26
(d) 19

Question 20: Select the related word/letters/number from the given alternatives

414 : 636 :: 325 : ?

(a) 222
(b) 636
(c) 547
(d) 414

Question 21: Select the related word/letters/number from the given alternatives

SNAKE : VQDNH :: CRADLE : ?

(a) EVFGOF
(b) FUDGOH

(c) EUDGOH
(d) FVDGPH

Question 22: Select the related word/letters/number from the given alternatives

$\sqrt{\text{AFI}}$: 13 :: $\sqrt{\text{DDA}}$: ?

(a) 22
(b) 12
(c) 21
(d) 24

Question 23: Select the related word/letters/number from the given alternatives.

FE : HG :: ML : ?

(a) QP
(b) PO
(c) JI
(d) ON

Question 24: Select the related word/letters/number from the given alternatives.

ACE : BDF :: MOQ : ?

(a) MZU
(b) MVT
(c) NPR
(d) NZV

Question 25: Select the related word/letters/number from the given alternatives.

8 : 23 :: 48 : ?

(a) 168

(b) 112

(c) 90

(d) 138

Question 26: Select the related word/letters/number from the given alternatives.

5 : 28 :: 8 : ?

(a) 25

(b) 67

(c) 40

(d) 64

Question 27: Select the related word/letters/number from the given alternatives.

CAT : 3120 :: MAT : ?

(a) 13120

(b) 12120

(c) 1312

(d) 10120

Question 28: Select the related word/letters/number from the given alternatives.

DEF : EFD :: FGH : ?

(a) FHG

(b) HGF

(c) HFG

(d) GHF

Question 29: Select the related word/letters/number from the given alternatives

RPKD : OKPG :: ESWK : ?

(a) HSWG
(b) BWSN
(c) BSWN
(d) HWSH

Question 30: Select the related word/letters/number from the given alternatives

ABCD : NPRT :: FGHI : ?

(a) KLMN
(b) OQRT
(c) RTUW
(d) SUWY

Question 31: Select the related word/letters/number from the given alternatives

UDBS : USBD :: PEAX : ?

(a) PXEA
(b) PXAE
(c) PEXA
(d) PAEX

Question 32: Select the related word/letters/number from the given alternatives

GRYD : YDGR :: EKSB : ?

(a) SKBE
(b) SBKE
(c) BSEK

(d) SBEK

Question 33: Select the related word/letters/number from the given alternatives

FILM : ADGH :: MILK : ?

(a) ADGF
(b) HDGE
(c) HDGF
(d) HEGF

Question 34: Select the related word/letters/number from the given alternatives

QPRS : TUWV :: JIKL : ?

(a) MNOP
(b) MNPO
(c) NMOP
(d) NMPO

Question 35: Select the related word/letters/number from the given alternatives

FJUL : BOQQ :: LHRX : ?

(a) BKPR
(b) MNCC
(c) HRYY
(d) HMNC

Question 36: Select the related word/letters/number from the given alternatives

EJOT : VQLG :: BGLQ : ?

(a) AEIM
(b) AFKP

(c) YTOJ
(d) ZUPK

Question 37: Select the related word/letters/number from the given alternatives

7584 : 5362 :: 4673 : ?

(a) 2367
(b) 2451
(c) 2531
(d) None of these

Question 38: Select the related word/letters/number from the given alternatives

2, 14, 16

(a) 2, 7, 8
(b) 2, 9, 16
(c) 3, 21, 24
(d) 4, 16, 18

Question 39: Select the related word/letters/number from the given alternatives

2 5 9 is related to 13 16 20, in the same way 1 4 8 is related to

(a) 31 61 02
(b) 12 15 20
(c) 21 25 29
(d) 12 15 19

Question 40: Select the related word/letters/number from the given alternatives

5 : 100 :: 7 : ?

(a) 49

(b) 196

(c) 91

(d) 98

Question 41: There is definite relationship between figures (1) and (2). Establish a similar relationship between figures (3) and (4) by choosing a suitable figure from the answer set.

Problem figures

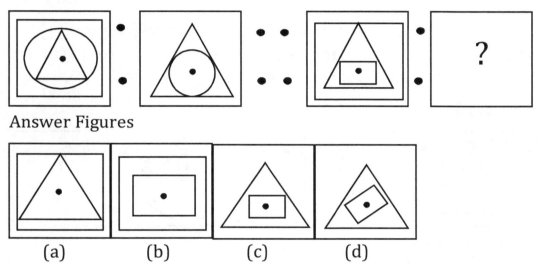

Answer Figures

(a)   (b)   (c)   (d)

Question42: There is definite relationship betweenfigures (1) and (2). Establish a similar relationship between figures (3) and (4) by choosing a suitable figure from the answer set.

Problem figures

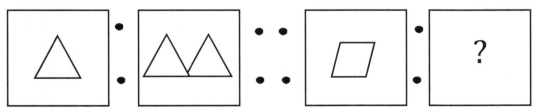

Answer Figures

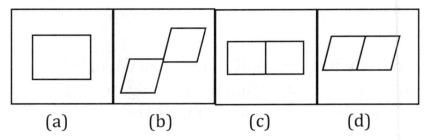

(a)　　　　　(b)　　　　　(c)　　　　　(d)

Question 43: There is definite relationship between figures (1) and (2). Establish a similar relationship between figures (3) and (4) by choosing a suitable figure from the answer set.

Problem figures

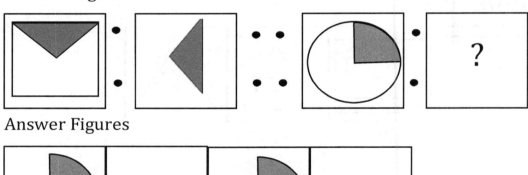

Answer Figures

(a)　　　　　(b)　　　　　(c)　　　　　(d)

Question 44: There is definite relationship between figures (1) and (2). Establish a similar relationship between figures (3) and (4) by choosing a suitable figure from the answer set.

Problem figures

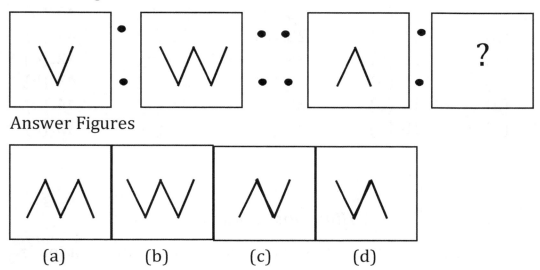

Answer Figures

    (a)   (b)   (c)   (d)

Question 45: There is definite relationship between figures (1) and (2). Establish a similar relationship between figures (3) and (4) by choosing a suitable figure from the answer set.

Problem figures

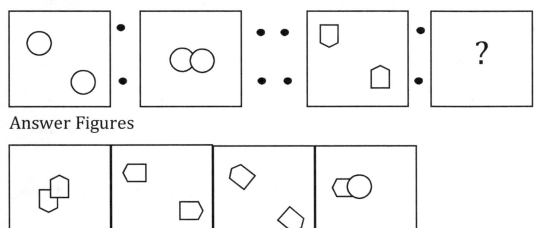

Answer Figures

Answers

1. (d)	10. (a)	19. (a)	28. (d)	37. (b)
2. (b)	11. (c)	20. (c)	29. (b)	38. (c)
3. (b)	12. (a)	21. (b)	30. (d)	39. (d)
4. (c)	13. (b)	22. (c)	31. (b)	40. (b)
5. (b)	14. (d)	23. (d)	32. (d)	41. (a)
6. (d)	15. (a)	24. (c)	33. (c)	42. (d)
7. (b)	16. (d)	25. (d)	34. (b)	43. (b)
8. (a)	17. (b)	26. (b)	35. (d)	44. (a)
9. (b)	18. (C)	27. (a)	36. (c)	45. (a)

Hints and solutions

1. As, Vacation is similar to Holiday, in the same way Vocation is similar to Career.

2. As waiter works at restaurant, in similar way lawyer works at court.

3. As sailor works at Ship, in similar way Artist works at Theatre.

4. As Engineer works on Site, in similar way Worker works at Factory.

5. As Farmer produces Crops, goldsmith produces Ornaments.

6. As author writes book, in similar way Editor edits Newspaper.

7. As Chef prepares food, in similar way choreographer teaches Ballet.

8. As Carpenter produces Furniture, in similar way Tailor stiches Clothes.

9. Cub is the young one of Lion.

10. Caterpillar is the young one of butterfly.

11. Wall is made up of bricks, in similar way shoes made up of leather.

12. As cloth is made of fibre, in similar way book is made of paper.

13. Oil is extracted from seed.

14. Butter came from Milk.

15. As play is performed by an actor. Similarly, Concert is performed by a musician.

16. As antonym of Right is Wrong. Similarly, antonym of Pleasure is Sad.

17. As Death is opposite to Life. Similarly End is opposite to Beginning.

18.   O   K   Z   X   D   Q
       ↓   ↓   ↓   ↓   ↓   ↓ [+1]
       P   L   A   Y   E   R

19. $8^2 = 64$. Similarly $17^2 = 289$.

20. $(3+2) = 5$; $(2+2) = 4$; $(5+2) = 7$.

21.   C   R   A   D   L   E
       ↓   ↓   ↓   ↓   ↓   ↓ [+3]
       F   U   D   G   O   H

22. $\sqrt{AFI} = \sqrt{169} = 13$. Similarly $\sqrt{DDA} = \sqrt{441} = 21$

23.   M   L
       ↓   ↓

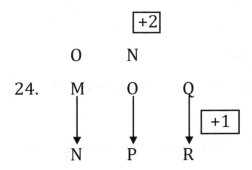

24.

$$
\begin{array}{ccc}
\text{M} & \text{O} & \text{Q} \\
\downarrow & \downarrow & \downarrow \boxed{+1} \\
\text{N} & \text{P} & \text{R}
\end{array}
$$

25. 8 x 6 = 48 ; 23 x 6 = 138

26. $5^2+3 = 28$. Similarly $8^2+3 = 67$.

27. As C is the 3rd letter, A is the 1st letter and T is the 20th letter. Similarly MAT = 13120

28.

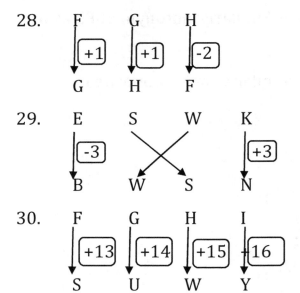

29.

$$
\begin{array}{cccc}
\text{E} & \text{S} & \text{W} & \text{K} \\
\downarrow \boxed{-3} & \searrow & \swarrow & \downarrow \boxed{+3} \\
\text{B} & \text{W} & \text{S} & \text{N}
\end{array}
$$

30.

$$
\begin{array}{cccc}
\text{F} & \text{G} & \text{H} & \text{I} \\
\downarrow \boxed{+13} & \downarrow \boxed{+14} & \downarrow \boxed{+15} & \downarrow \boxed{+16} \\
\text{S} & \text{U} & \text{W} & \text{Y}
\end{array}
$$

31. 1st and 3rd letter remain constant. 2nd and 4th letter gets interchanged. So PEAX is coded as PXAE.

32. 1st and 3rd letters interchanged. 2nd and 4th letters interchanged. So ESKB is coded as SBEK.

33. Each letter of the first group is moved five steps backwards to obtain the corresponding letter of the second group.

34. The first and fourth letters of the first group are each moved three steps forward while the second and fourth letters are each moved five steps forward to obtain the corresponding letters of the second group.

35. The first and third letters of the first group are each moved four steps backward while the second and fourth letters are each moved five steps forward to obtain the corresponding letters of the second group.

36. Each letter of the first group occupies the same position from the beginning of the alphabet as the corresponding letter of the second group occupies from the end of the alphabet.

37. 7584 – 2222 = 5362 ; 4673 – 2222 = 2451

38. The pattern is as follows.

   2nd number = 1st number x 7 and

   3rd number = 1st number x 8

Therefore, the required triplet is 3, 21, 24.

39.

12   15   19

40. For 5 $\longrightarrow$ 5^2x4 = 100. Similarly, for 7 $\longrightarrow$ 7^2x4 = 196.

41. From figure (1) and (2), the outermost figure disappears while innermost dot remains at its position. But the remaining two figures interchange places. Similar pattern is followed between figure (3) and (4).

42. In the first pair, the triangle is replaced by rhombus. In the same way, in the second pair, both triangles will be replaced by two rhombus.

43. In the first pair, the shaded part becomes the second figure by rotating 90° in clockwise direction.

44. In the first pair, the first figure is doubled to make the second figure. In the same way, in the second pair, the figure will be doubled.

45. In the first pair, the first figure is merged to make the second figure. In the same way, in the second pair, the figure will be merged.

Mirror and Water images

Introduction:

Mirror Image: It's obtained by Placing a Mirror in front of the real figure. The reflection of images on mirror is called Mirror Image.

In the Mirror image of an object, the Lower and upper parts

remains constant whereas LHS and RHS gets interchanged, means Left part of an object becomes Right part and Right part becomes the Left part.

EXAMPLE 1

Question Figure.

Answer Figures

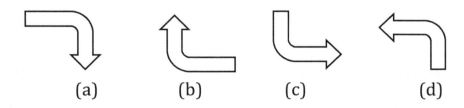

(a)　　　(b)　　　(c)　　　(d)

Ans: (d)

Explanation: The right side arrow in the question is turned into Left side. Thus the answer is (d)

EXAMPLE 2

Chose the correct image of the figure

Answer Figures

(a)   (b)   (c)   (d)

Ans: (b)

Explanation: (b) is the correct mirror image of the above figure as the LHS moved to RHS.

EXAMPLE 3

Chose the correct image of the figure.

Answer Figures

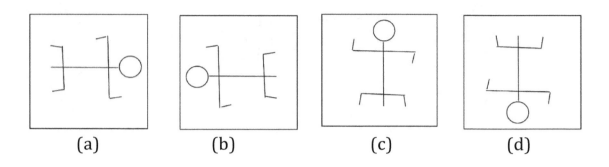

(a) (b) (c) (d)

Ans: (c)

Explanation: (c) is the correct answer as the RHS and LHS get interchanged.

Water Image:

The reflection of an object into the is called water image. It's obtained by inverting an object vertically.

EXAMPLE 1

Question Figure

Answer Figure

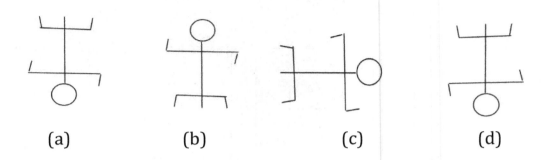

(a)   (b)   (c)   (d)

Ans: (a)

Explanation: Ans (a) shows the correct water image as that the image is inversed and the upside hand show as downside and vice-versa.

Exercise

Question 1: Which of the answer figure is exactly the mirror image of the given figure, when the mirror is held on the line AB?

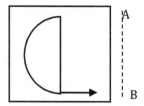

Answer Figures

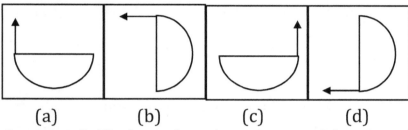

    (a)   (b)   (c)   (d)

Question 2: Find out the mirror image of the given figure.

Answer Figures

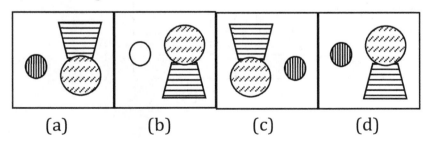

    (a)   (b)   (c)   (d)

Question 3: Find out the mirror image of the given figure.

Answer Figures

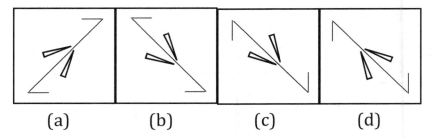

(a)   (b)   (c)   (d)

Question 4: Find out the mirror image of the given figure.

Answer figure

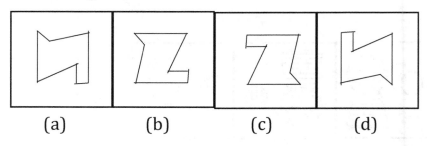

(a)   (b)   (c)   (d)

Question 5: Find out the mirror image of the given figure.

Answer Figure

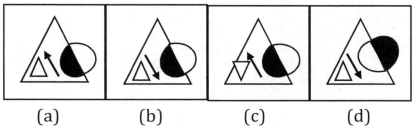

| (a) | (b) | (c) | (d) |

Question 6: Find out the mirror image of the given figure.

Answer Figure

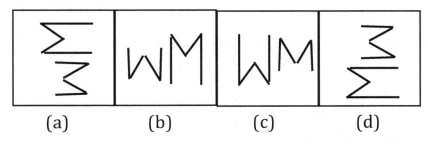

| (a) | (b) | (c) | (d) |

Question 7: Find out the water image of the given figure.

Answer Figure

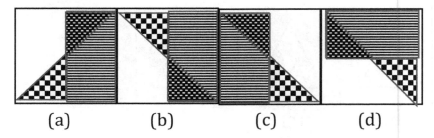

(a)　　　　　　(b)　　　　　　(c)　　　　　　(d)

Question 8: Find out the water image of the given figure.

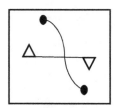

Answer Figure

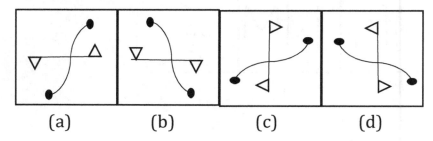

(a)　　　　　　(b)　　　　　　(c)　　　　　　(d)

Answers

1. (d)	4. (a)	7. (c)
2. (d)	5. (a)	8. (a)
3. (d)	6. (b)	

Counting of Figures

Introduction:

Counting of figures is realization of simple geometrical plane figures from a complex figure. It is designed to test the ability and logical approach of the students. The figures which are asked for counting can be straight line, triangle, square, rectangle, polygon etc.

To find the accurate answer for these question, firstly, students needs to find the required figures formed by individual section of figure, then the figure formed by combination of two figure and so on.

EXAMPLE 1

How many triangles are there in the given question figure?

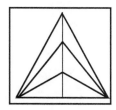

(a) 15   (b) 14   (c) 16   (d) 20

Ans: (a)

Explanation:

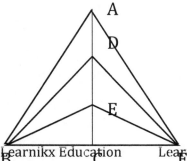

Hence, Such number of triangles are as follows

Δ ABC, Δ AFB, Δ AFC, Δ ABD, Δ ADC, Δ DFB, Δ DFC, Δ EFB, Δ EFC, ΔDBC, Δ EBC, Δ DCE, Δ DBE, Δ ABE, Δ ACE = 15 triangles.

Exercise

Question 1: How many rectangles are there in the given figure?

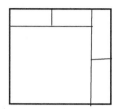

(a) 6
(b) 7
(c) 8
(d) 9

Question 2: How many squares are there in the given figure?

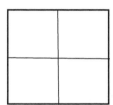

(a) 4
(b) 5
(c) 6
(d) 7

Question 3: How many triangles are there in the following figure?

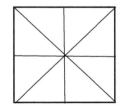

(a) 16
(b) 12
(c) 10
(d) 8

Question 4: How many numbers of squares in the following figures?

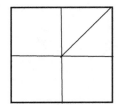

(a) 6
(b) 8
(c) 5
(d) 10

Question 5: How many triangles are there in the following figure?

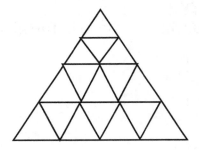

(a) 29
(b) 27
(c) 23
(d) 30

Question 6: What is the number of straight lines in the following?

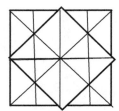

(a) 11
(b) 14
(c) 16
(d) 17

Question 7: How many triangles are there in the following figure?

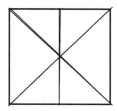

(a) 6
(b) 8
(c) 10
(d) 12

Answer

1. (c)
2. (b)
3. (a)
4. (c)

5. (b)
6. (b)
7. (d)

1.

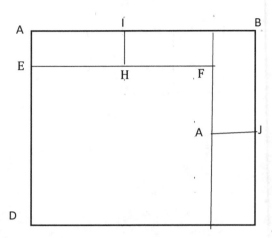

Required rectangles

AIHE, ILFH, ALFE, LBJK, JCGK, LBGG, EPGD, ABCD. Hence, required rectangles = 8.

2.

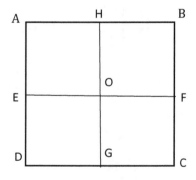

There are 5 squares in the figure namely AHOE, HOFB, FOGC, OGDE, ABCD.

3.

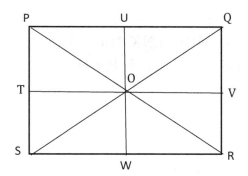

Name of the triangles in the present figure are POU, UOQ, QOV, VOR, ROW, WOS, SOT, TOP, SOP, POQ, QOR, ROS, SPR, QPR, SQP, SQR

4.

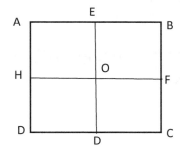

Name of the squares are AEOH, EBFO, HOGD, OFGC, ABCD. Hence there are 5 squares in this figure.

5.

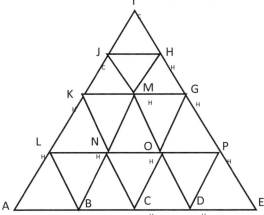

The triangles are JHI, KMJ, MHJ, MGH, LNK, NMK, NOM, OGM, OFG, ABL, BNL, BCN, CON, CDO, DFO, DEF, IKL, ILF, IAE, ACK, ADI, EGC, EBH, BMD, KGC, NHF, LOJ.

6.

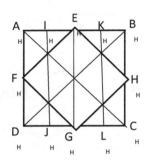

There are 14 straight lines in this figure namely AB, BC, DC, AD, AC,BD,EG, FH, EF, FG, GH, EH, IJ, KL.

7.

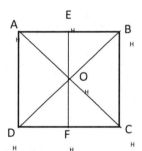

There are 12 triangles in the figure namely AOE, EOB, AOD, DOF, FOC, BOC, ABD, BCD, ACD, ABC, AOB, DOC.

Word Formation

Introduction:

It is a technique of making new meaningful words using the letters of give word. In word formation a letter is used only once to form a new word from the letters of given word.

Type I – Word Formation using the given word

EXAMPLE 1

Form the given Options, select the word which cannot be formed using the letters of the given word?

PSYCHOLOGY

(a) School
(b) Look
(c) Pool
(d) Holy

Ans: (b)

Explanation: 'LOOK' cannot be formed by letters using the given word, as the alphabet 'K' is not present in 'PSYCHOLOGY'.

EXAMPLE 2

Form the given Options, select the word which cannot be formed using the letters of the given word?

HISTORICAL

(a) Trophy
(b) Chariot

(c) Chart
(d) Chaos

Ans: (a)

Explanation: 'TROPHY' cannot be formed by using the letters given in the word, because alphabets 'P' and 'Y' not available in the word 'HISTORICAL'

EXAMPLE 3

Form the given Options, select the word which cannot be formed using the letters of the given word?

CAPTURED

(a) Cap
(b) Red
(c) Cat
(d) Turn

Ans: (d)

Explanation: 'TURN' cannot be formed by using the alphabets given in the word, because 'N' is missing in the word 'CAPTURED'.

Type II – Forming words using Jumbled words.

Introduction:

In it, set of English alphabets will be given in an jumbled order, from that a meaningful Word have to be formed.

EXAMPLE 4

Find the correct Sequence

F R B O E E

1 2 3 4 5 6

(a) 1,5,3,2,6,4
(b) 3,6,1,4,6,2
(c) 3,5,1,4,2,5
(d) 3,5,4,1,2,6

Ans: (c)

Explanation: B E F O R E

3 5 1 4 2 5

Exercise

Question 1: Form the given Options, select the word which cannot be formed using the letters of the given word?

PUNISHMENT

(a) Net
(b) Put
(c) Push
(d) Name

Question 2: Form the given Options, select the word which cannot be formed using the letters of the given word?

CORRESPONDENCE

(a) Condense
(b) Respond
(c) Correspond
(d) Respondent

Question 3: Form the given Options, select the word which cannot be formed using the letters of the given word?

INTERVENTION

(a) Enter
(b) Intention
(c) Invention
(d) Entertain

Question 4: Form the given Options, select the word which cannot be formed using the letters of the given word?

COMMUNICATION

(a) Union
(b) Action
(c) Music
(d) Caution

Question 5: Form the given Options, select the word which cannot be formed using the letters of the given word?

CONSOLIDATE

(a) Solid
(b) Coin
(c) Link
(d) Detail

Question 6: Form the given Options, select the word which cannot be formed using the letters of the given word?

GRASSHOPPER

(a) Hope
(b) Rope
(c) Soap
(d) Gram

Question 7: Form the given Options, select the word which can be formed using the letters of the given word?

IMMEASURABLE

(a) Meat
(b) Bible
(c) Bail
(d) Red

Question 8: Form the given Options, select the word which can be formed using the letters of the given word?

ENVIRONMENT

(a) Virus
(b) Movement
(c) Exit
(d) Eminent

Question 9: Form the given Options, select the word which can be formed using the letters of the given word?

COMPANIONSHIP

(a) Opinion
(b) Nation
(c) Open
(d) Opium

Question 10: Form the given Options, select the word which can be formed using the letters of the given word?

PREPARATION

(a) Pamper
(b) Repeat
(c) Partition
(d) Parrot

Question 11: Form the given Options, select the word which can be formed using the letters of the given word?

MEASUREMENT

(a) Master
(b) Mantle
(c) Summit
(d) Assure

Question 12: Form the given Options, select the word which can be formed using the letters of the given word?

EXAMINATION

(a) Animal
(b) Examiner
(c) National
(d) Animation

Question 13: Form the given Options, select the word which can be formed using the letters of the given word?

RHINOCEROS

(a) Renal
(b) Hind
(c) Sure
(d) Horse

Question 14: Form the given Options, select the word which can be formed using the letters of the given word?

PRAGMATIC

(a) Guitar
(b) Mark
(c) Game
(d) Magic

Question 15: Form the given Options, select the word which can be formed using the letters of the given word?

VENTURESOME

(a) Event
(b) Truth
(c) Rose
(d) Rental

Question 16: Form the given Options, select the word which cannot be formed using the letters of the given word?

INFLATIONARY

(a) Flair
(b) Faulty
(c) National
(d) Ration

Question 17: Form the given Options, select the word which cannot be formed using the letters of the given word?

THUNDERBOLT

(a) Bend
(b) Hunter
(c) Bother
(d) Bowled

Question 18: Form the given Options, select the word which can be formed using the letters of the given word?

PENINSULA

(a) Insulin
(b) Pencil
(c) Last
(d) Nine

Question 19: Form the given Options, select the word which cannot be formed using the letters of the given word?

ADVANTAGEOUS

(a) Stage
(b) Gate
(c) Danger
(d) Sad

Question 20: Form the given Options, select the word which can be formed using the letters of the given word?

DISAGREEMENT

(a) Mint
(b) Tent
(c) Mistake
(d) Deed

Question 21: Form the given Options, select the word which can be formed using the letters of the given word?

GUARANTEED

(a) Deed
(b) Weed
(c) Seed
(d) Need

Question 22: Form the given Options, select the word which can be formed using the letters of the given word?

VULNERABLE

(a) Viable
(b) Ball
(c) Table
(d) Nil

Question 23: Find the meaningful Sequence.

G O L B O I Y

1 2 3 4 5 6 7

(a) 1,2,3,6,4,5,7
(b) 4,6,5,3,2,1,7
(c) 4,6,7,2,1,3,5
(d) 4,5,6,3,2,1,7

Question 24: Find the meaningful Sequence.

A T E T L M P E

1 2 3 4 5 6 7 8

(a) 2,3,6,7,5,1,4,8
(b) 1,2,3,6,8,4,5,7
(c) 1,2,4,8,6,7,5,3
(d) 4,8,6,7,5,3,1,2

Question 25: Find the correct Sequence.

N I M E A J S

1 2 3 4 5 6 7

(a) 7,6,1,4,2,5,3
(b) 6,5,7,3,2,1,4
(c) 3,2,7,5,4,1,6
(d) 5,7,3,6,1,4,2

Question 26: Find the correct Sequence.

R O N G A K O A

1 23 4567 8

(a) 6,8,3,4,5,7,1,2
(b) 6,8,3,4,5,1,2,7
(c) 1,2,4,8,7,6,5,3
(d) 6,8,4,2,7,1,3,5

Answers

1. (d)	8. (d)	15. (c)	22. (b)
2. (d)	9. (a)	16. (b)	23. (b)
3. (d)	10. (d)	17. (d)	24. (a)
4. (c)	11. (a)	18. (d)	25. (b)
5. (c)	12. (d)	19. (c)	26. (b)
6. (d)	13. (d)	20. (a)	
7. (c)	14. (d)	21. (d)	

Hints and solutions

1. 'NAME' cannot be formed by using the alphabets given in the word, as the alphabet 'A' is missing in the word 'PUNISHMENT'

2. 'RESPONDENT' cannot be formed using the alphabets given in the word, as the alphabet 'T' is Missing in the word 'CORRESPONDENCE'

3. 'ENTERTAIN' cannot be formed using the alphabets in the given word, as the alphabet 'A' is not present in the word 'INTERVENTION'

4. 'MUSIC' cannot be formed using the alphabets in the given word, as the alphabet 'S' is missing in the word 'COMMUNICATION'

5. 'LINK' cannot be formed using the alphabets given in the word, as the alphabet 'K' is missing in the word 'CONSOLIDATE'

6. As the alphabet 'M' is missing in the word ' GRASSHOPPER', the word 'GRAM' cannot be formed.

7. Word 'BAIL' can be formed form the main word 'IMMEASURABLE'.

8. Word 'EMINENT' can be formed from the main word 'ENVIRONMENT'

9. Word ' OPINION' can be formed using the main word ' CAMPANIONSHIP'

10. Word 'PARROT' can be formed using the main word 'PREPERATION'

11. Word 'MASTER' can be formed from the main word 'MEASUREMENT'

12. Word 'ANIMATION' can be formed from the main word 'EXAMINATION'

13. Word 'HORSE' can be formed from the main word 'RHINOCEROS'

14. Word ' MAGIC' Can be formed from the main word 'PRAGMATIC'

15. Word 'ROSE' can be formed from the main word 'VENTURESOME'

16. Word ' FAULTY' cannot be formed from the main word 'INFLATIONARY', as the alphabet 'U' is missing.

17. Word 'BOWLED' cannot be formed from the main word 'THUNDERBOLT', as the alphabet 'W' is missing in it.

18. Word ' NINE' can be formed from the main word ' PENINSULA'

19. Word 'DANGER' cannot be formed from the main word 'ADVANTAGEOUS'.

20. Word 'MINT' can be formed from the main word 'DISAGREEMENT'

21. Word 'NEED' can be formed from the main word 'GUARANTEED'.

22. Word 'BALL' can be formed using the main word 'VULNERABLE'.

23.
B I O L O G Y
4 6 5 3 2 1 7

24.
T E M P L A T E
2 3 6 7 5 1 4 8

25.
J A S M I N E
6 5 7 3 2 1 4

26.
K A N G A R O O
6 8 3 4 5 1 2 7

Number Series

Introduction:

In number series, numbers are arranged in a particular Sequence using some basic mathematical or logical operations.

A logically arranged Sequence of number is called Series.

Some of the examples of Operations are as follows

- Prime numbers
- Odd number and Even numbers
- Square and Square roots of a number
- Cube and cube roots of a number
- Combination of the above operations

Type I – Find out the next number or missing number

In it, a sequence of number will be given, you have to find the next or missing number in the sequence by understanding how the sequence is formed.

EXAMPLE 1

Find out the next number?

1,2,4,8,16,?

(a) 18
(b) 32
(c) 64
(d) 30

Ans: (b)

Explanation: 1x2 =2; 2x2 =4; 4x2 =8; 8x2 =16; 16x2 =32.

EXAMPLE 2

Find the next number?

11,13,17,19,23,?

(a) 27
(b) 25
(c) 29
(d) 31

Ans: (c)

Explanation:11,13,17,19,23 are prime numbers. So the next Prime number is 29.

EXAMPLE 3

Find the next number?

1,3,6,10,15,?

(a) 20
(b) 18
(c) 17
(d) 21

Ans: (d)

Explanation: 1+2=3 ; 3+3=6 ; 6+4=10 ; 10+5=15 ; 15+6=21.

Type II – Find the wrong number

In this, a sequence of numbers will be given and a number doesn't form part of that sequence. You have to find that wrong number in the sequence.

EXAMPLE 4

Find the wrong number

9,14,19,25,32,40

(a) 14
(b) 25
(c) 32
(d) 9

Ans: (d)

Explanation: 40-8= 32; 32-7=25; 25-6=19; 19-5=14; 14-4=10. So, the number is 9 is the wrong number in the sequence.

EXAMPLE 5

Find the wrong number

4,10,22,46,96,190,382

(a) 4
(b) 10
(c) 96
(d) 382

Ans: (c)

Explanation: (4x2)+2= 10, (10x2)+2=22, (22x2)+2=46, (46x2)+2=94, (94x2)+2=190, (190x2)+2=382. So the wrong number is 96.

Exercise

Question 1: Find the next number?

5,10,20,25,35,40,?

(a) 50
(b) 55
(c) 60
(d) 65

Question 2: Find the next number?

1,4,10,22,46,?

(a) 92
(b) 94
(c) 100
(d) 104

Question 3: Find the missing number?

10,10,20,70,?,2030?

(a) 140
(b) 340
(c) 100
(d) 180

Question 4:Find the next number?

3,7,13,27,53,?

(a) 107
(b) 105
(c) 106
(d) 104

Question 5: Find the missing number.

50,110,180,260,?,450.

(a) 360
(b) 350
(c) 390
(d) 320

Question 6: Find the missing number?

1,2,4,5,10,11,22,?,46

(a) 45
(b) 44
(c) 23
(d) 24

Question 7: Find the next number.

6,13,28,59,?

(a) 111
(b) 112
(c) 121

(d) 122

Question 8: Find the missing number?

13,25,39,?,73

(a) 55
(b) 45
(c) 62
(d) 61

Question 9: Find the missing number?

1,1,2,3,5,8,?,21

(a) 12
(b) 13
(c) 15
(d) 14

Question 10: Find the missing number

2,4,16,?,65536

(a) 32
(b) 244
(c) 256
(d) 64

Question 11: Find the next number?

54,26,12,?

(a) 4
(b) 3
(c) 2
(d) 5

Question 12: Find the missing number

36,34,30,28,24,?

(a) 20
(b) 22
(c) 23
(d) 26

Question 13: Find the wrong number

121,143,165,186,209

(a) 143
(b) 165
(c) 186
(d) 209

Question 14: Find the wrong number.

125,126,124,127,123,129

(a) 126
(b) 124
(c) 123

(d) 129

Question 15: Find the wrong number

1,2,6,12,36,70,216

(a) 36
(b) 70
(c) 216
(d) 12

Question 16: Find the Wrong number

1,3,6,10,14,21

(a) 14
(b) 10
(c) 21
(d) 10

Question 17: Find the wrong number

1,2,3,5,7,11,13

(a) 2
(b) 1
(c) 5
(d) 11

Question 18: Find the Wrong number

49,42,36,28,21,14

(a) 21
(b) 28
(c) 36
(d) 49

Question 19: Find the wrong number

19,38,57,77,95

(a) 57
(b) 77
(c) 95
(d) 38

Question 20: Find the Wrong number

11,8,13,9,5

(a) 9
(b) 5
(c) 13
(d) 11

Question 21: Find the Wrong number

30,900,33,1089,36,1306,39,1521

(a) 900
(b) 1089
(c) 1306

(d) 1521

Question 22: Find the wrong number

4,6,16,54,244

(a) 54
(b) 16
(c) 244
(d) 6

Question 23: Find the wrong number

4,9,16,25,36,49,66,81,100

(a) 25
(b) 49
(c) 81
(d) 66

Question 24: Find the wrong number

210,175,141,108,77,45

(a) 77
(b) 108
(c) 49
(d) 175

Question 25: Find the wrong number

8,4,2,1,¾, ¼.

(a) 1
(b) ¾
(c) ¼
(d) 2

Question 26: Find the missing number

64,67,73,82,?

(a) 90
(b) 94
(c) 83
(d) 95

Question 27:Find the missing number

343,345,349,357,?

(a) 367
(b) 373
(c) 413
(d) 716

Question 28: Find the missing number

3,3,6,18,72,?

(a) 630
(b) 360
(c) 180

(d) 420

Question 29: Find the missing number

8, 16, 64, 384, ?

(a) 3027
(b) 2072
(c) 3072
(d) 4017

Question 30: Find the missing number

63,65,68,73,80, ?

(a) 95
(b) 91
(c) 89
(d) 105

Question 31: Find the missing number

11, 122, 344, 677, 1121, ?

(a) 1766
(b) 2458
(c) 1676
(d) 1898

Question 32: Find the missing number

420,457,504,541, ?

(a) 641
(b) 613
(c) 688
(d) 588

Question 33: Find the missing number

46, 51, 106, 661, ?

(a) 6216
(b) 7819
(c) 7141
(d) 1047

Question 34: Find the missing number

43, 54, 76, 109, 153, ?

(a) 802
(b) 208
(c) 210
(d) 415

Answers

1. (a)	9. (b)	17. (b)	25. (b)	33. (a)
2. (b)	10. (c)	18. (C)	26. (b)	34. (b)
3. (b)	11. (d)	19. (b)	27. (b)	
4. (a)	12. (b)	20. (a)	28. (b)	
5. (b)	13. (c)	21. (c)	29. (c)	
6. (c)	14. (d)	22. (c)	30. (b)	
7. (d)	15. (b)	23. (d)	31. (c)	
8. (a)	16. (a)	24. (a)	32. (d)	

Hints and solutions

1. 5+5=10 ; 10+10=20 ; 20+5=25 ; 25+10=35 ; 35+5=40 ; 40+10=50.

2. (1x2)+2=4; (4x2)+2=10; (10x2)+2=22; (22x2)+2=46; (46x2)+2=94.

3. (10x2)-10=10; (10x3)-10=20; (20x4)-10=70; (70x5)-10=340; (340x6)-10=2030.

4. (3x2)+1=7; (7x2)-1=13; (13x2)+1=27; (27x2)-1=53; (53x2)+1=107.

5. 50+60=110; 110+70=180; 180+80=260; 260+90=350; 350+100=450.

6. 1+1=2; 2x2=4; 4+1=5; 5x2=10; 10+1=11; 11x2=22; 22+1=23; 23x2=46.

7. (6x2)+1= 13; (13x2)+2=28; (28x2)+3=59; (59x2)+4=122

8. 13+12=25; 25+14=39; 39+16=55; 55+18=73.

9. 1+1=2; 1+2=3, 2+3=5, 3+5=8, 5+8=13, 8+13=21.

10. 22=4, 42=16, 162=256, 2562=65536

11. (54÷2)-1=26; (26÷2)-1=12; (12÷2)-1=5.

12. 36-2=34, 34-4=30, 30-2=28, 28-4=24, 24-2=22.

13. 121+22=143, 143+22=165, 165+22=187, 187+22=209. So the wrong number is 186.

14. In this sequence, the operation are interchanged one after another like +1, -2, +3, -4, +5.So, 125+1= 126, 126-2=124, 124+3=127, 127-4=123, 123+5= 128.So, 129 is the wrong number.

15. 1x2=2, 2x3=6, 6x2=12, 12x3=36, 36x2=72, 72x3=216. So the wrong number is 70.

16. 1+2=3, 3+3=6, 6+4=10, 10+5=15, 15+6=21. So, the wrong number is 14.

17. All the number in the Sequence are Prime numbers, except the number 1.

18. All the numbers are divisible by 7, except the number 36.

19. All the numbers are divisible by 19, except the number 77.

20. 11-3=8, 8+5=13, 13-3=10, 10+5=15. So the wrong number is 9.

21. The 2nd number in the sequence is the square value of the first number. That 302=900, 332=1089, 362=1296,392=1521.So the number 1306 is wrong number.

22. $(4+2) \times 1 = 6$, $(6+2) \times 2 = 16$, $(16+2) \times 3 = 54$, $(54+2) \times 4 = 224$. So the wrong number is 244.

23. $22=4, 32=9, 42=16, 52=25, 62=36, 72=49, 82=64, 92=81, 102=100$. So the wrong number is 66.

24. $210-35=175$, $175-34=141$, $141-33=108$, $108-32=76$, $76-31=45$. So the wrong number is 77.

25. $8 \times \frac{1}{2} = 4$, $4 \times \frac{1}{2} = 2$, $2 \times \frac{1}{2} = 1$, $1 \times \frac{1}{2} = \frac{1}{2}$, $\frac{1}{2} \times \frac{1}{2} = \frac{1}{4}$. So the wrong number is $\frac{3}{4}$.

26. $64+3=67$; $67+6=73$; $73+9=82$; $82+12=94$.

27. $343+2=345$; $345+4=349$; $349+8=355$; $355+16=373$

28. $3 \times 1=3$; $3 \times 2=6$; $6 \times 3=18$; $18 \times 4=72$; $72 \times 5=360$

29. $8 \times 2=16$; $16 \times 4=64$; $64 \times 6=384$; $384 \times 8=3072$

30. $63+2=65$; $65+3=68$; $68+5=73$; $73+7=80$; $80+11=91$

31. $11+111=122$; $122+222=344$; $344+333=677$; $677+444=1121$; $1121+555=1676$

32. $420+37=457$; $457+47=504$; $504+37=541$; $541+47=588$

33. $46+5=51$; $51+55=106$; $106+555=661$; $661+555=6216$

34. $43+11=54$; $54+22=76$; $76+33=109$; $109+44=153$; $153+55=208$.

Logical Sequencing

Introduction:

Logical Sequencing is the arrangement of words in a universally accepted way.

In it certain pre-linked words are given and numbered, followed by various sequence of the numbers denoting them, as options. Students are required to arrange these words in a logical sequence based on a common property and then choose the correct sequence from the given options.

Types of logical Sequencing

- Sequence of occurrence of events or various stages in a process
- Sequence of objects in a class or group
- Sequence in ascending or descending order
- Sequential order of words according to dictionary

Type I- Sequence of occurrence of events or various stages in a process.

> The given words may be related to an event or a chainprocess from beginning to end. Students are required to choose that correct option, which represents the logical sequence of process.

EXAMPLE 1

Arrange the following words in a logical sequence.

1. Application
2. Selection
3. Exam
4. Interview
5. Advertisement

Options:

(a) 1,2,3,4,5
(b) 5,1,3,4,2
(c) 5,3,1,4,2
(d) 4,5,1,2,3

Ans: (b)

Explanation: For a Job, Advertisement is the 1st stage- 5, Application is the 2nd stage - 1, Exam is the 3rd stage- 3, Interview is the 4th stage –4, Selection is the final stage – 2. So, the correct sequence is 5,1,3,4,2.

EXAMPLE 2

Identify the correct logic sequence.

1. Rainbow
2. Rain
3. Sun
4. Happy
5. Child

Options:

(a) 2,1,4,3,5

(b) 2,3,1,5,4
(c) 4,2,3,5,1
(d) 4,5,1,2,3

Ans: (b)

Explanation: Rain Stops–2, Sun Comes–3, Rainbow comes – 1, Children plays –5, Creates Happiness – 4. So, the correct sequence is 2,3,1,5,4

EXAMPLE 3

Identify the correct logic sequence.

1. Curd
2. Butter
3. Milk
4. Cow

Options:

(a) 4,3,1,2
(b) 4,3,2,1
(c) 4,1,3,2
(d) 1,3,2,4

Ans: (a)

Explanation: Cow – 4, gives milk – 3, milk formed as curd –1, gets butter from curd – 2.

Type II – Sequence of objects in a Class or Group

Sometimes words may be given such that they are related to a particular class or a group. Students are required to choose the option from the given alternatives, which shows the correct logical sequence of the objects in a particular class or group.

EXAMPLE 1

Arrange the following words in a meaningful order.

1. Sydney
2. Universe
3. World
4. Australia

Options:

(a) 2,4,3,1
(b) 4,1,3,2
(c) 1,2,3,4
(d) 1,4,3,2

Ans: (d)

Explanation: Sydney is a city situated in the country Australia. Australia is part of the World and world in turn, is part of the universe. So, the correct sequence is

   Sydney – Australia –World – Universe

The sequence is 1,4,3,2.

Type III – Sequence in Ascending or descending

The items or objects represented by the given words may be related to each other items of their properties. Students are required to arrange the given words on the increasing or decreasing order of their size,age,need,value, intensity etc.

EXAMPLE 1

Arrange the following words in a logical sequence.

1. Gold
2. Iron
3. Sand
4. Platinum
5. Diamond

Options:

(a) 2,4,3,5,1
(b) 3,2,1,5,4
(c) 4,5,1,3,2
(d) 5,4,3,2,1

Ans: (b)

Explanation: All the given words represent substances which can be arranged in the increasing order of their cost. The least cost is sand after which comes the cost of iron, followed by gold, diamond and the costliest among all is platinum. So, they can be arranged in a logical order as 3-2-1-5-4.

Type IV –Sequential order of words Ascending according to dictionary.

In this type of questions, Students are required to choose that option from the given alternatives, which is having the correct sequential order of the words according to English dictionary.

To check the order of each words in English dictionary, first of all check the forts letter of each word to find which among these comes first in English alphabet followed by the second letter and so on. The word whose letter comes first in English alphabet comes first, the word whose letter comes second in English alphabet comes second and so on.

EXAMPLE

Arrange the following words according to English dictionary.

1. Flower
2. Autumn
3. Automatic
4. Friday

Options:

(a) 3,4,2,1
(b) 3,2,1,4
(c) 2,3,1,4
(d) 4,3,2,1

Ans: (b)

Explanation: According to English dictionary, Automatic comes first, followed by Autumn which in turn followed by Flower and the last will be Friday. So, the correct sequential order is Automatic – Autumn –Flower – Friday.

Exercise

Question 1:Arrange the words in the sequence in which they occur in the dictionary.

1. Joke
2. Journalist
3. Joystick
4. Jockey

Options:

(a) 4,1,2,3
(b) 4,1,3,2
(c) 1,3,2,4
(d) 2,4,1,3

Question 2: Arrange the following words in ascending order.

1. Centimetre
2. Kilometre
3. Decimetre
4. Meter

Options:

(a) 3,1,2,4
(b) 4,2,1,3
(c) 1,3,4,2
(d) 2,4,3,1

Question 3: which one of the given responses would be a meaningful order of the following?

1. House
2. Palace
3. Bungalow
4. Hut

Options:

(a) 3,2,1,4
(b) 4,1,3,2
(c) 1,2,3,4
(d) 2,3,1,4

Question 4: which one of the given responses would be a meaningful order of the following?

1. Reading
2. Listening
3. Writing
4. Speaking

Options:

(a) 4,2,1,3
(b) 2,4,3,1
(c) 2,4,1,3
(d) 4,3,2,1

Question 5: which one of the given responses would be a meaningful order of the following?

1. Curd
2. Milk
3. Buttermilk
4. Cow
5. Ghee
6. Butter

Options:

(a) 2,5,6,4,1,3
(b) 4,6,2,1,3,5
(c) 4,2,1,3,6,5
(d) 2,6,4,5,3,1

Question 6:which one of the given responses would be a meaningful order of the following in ascending order?

1. Sending
2. Encoding
3. Receiving
4. Decoding

Options:

(a) 2,4,3,1
(b) 4,2,1,3
(c) 1,2,3,4
(d) 2,1,3,4

Question 7: Arrange the following words as per order in the English dictionary.

1. Important
2. Impart
3. Improvise
4. Improve

Options:

(a) 1,2,3,4
(b) 2,1,4,3
(c) 3,4,1,2
(d) 2,1,3,4

Question 8:Arrange the following words as per order in the English dictionary

1. Aqueous
2. Aquarium
3. Aquiline
4. Aquatic

Options:

(a) 4,3,2,1
(b) 1,2,3,4
(c) 2,4,1,3
(d) 3,1,4,2

Question 9:Which one of the following would be a meaningful order of the following words in a ascending order?

1. Income
2. Status
3. Education
4. Well-being
5. Job

Options:

(a) 1,3,25,4
(b) 1,2,5,3,4
(c) 3,1,5,2,4
(d) 3,5,1,2,4

Question 10: Which one of the following would be a meaningful order of the following words in a ascending order?

1. Weekly
2. Daily
3. Monthly
4. Fortnightly
5. Bimonthly

Options:

(a) 1,4,3,2,5
(b) 2,1,4,3,5
(c) 4,1,2,3,5
(d) 5,1,2,3,4

Question 11: Arrange the following words as per order in dictionary.

1. Ambitious
2. Ambiguous
3. Ambiguity
4. Animation
5. Animals

Options:

(a) 3,2,4,1,5
(b) 3,2,5,4,1
(c) 3,2,1,5,4
(d) 3,2,4,5,1

Question 12: Arrange the following words as per order in dictionary.

1. Billion
2. Bifurcate
3. Bilateral
4. Billiards

Options:

(a) 4,3,2,1
(b) 2,3,4,1
(c) 1,4,2,3
(d) 3,4,1,2

Question 13:Identify the correct logic sequence.

1. Study
2. Job
3. Examination
4. Earn
5. Apply

Options:

(a) 1,2,3,4,5
(b) 1,3,2,4,5
(c) 1,3,5,4,2
(d) 1,3,5,2,4

Question 14:Identify the correct logic sequence.

1. Index
2. Contents
3. Title
4. Chapters
5. Introduction

Options:

(a) 3,2,5,1,4
(b) 2,3,4,5,1
(c) 5,1,4,2,3
(d) 3,2,5,4,1

Question 15: Identify the correct logic sequence.

1. House
2. Street
3. Room
4. Town
5. District

Options:

(a) 3,2,1,4,5
(b) 3,1,4,2,5
(c) 3,1,2,4,5
(d) 3,1,2,5,4

Question 16:Identify the correct logic sequence.

1. Vegetable
2. Market
3. Cutting
4. Cooking
5. Food

Options:

(a) 1,2,3,4,5
(b) 2,1,3,4,5
(c) 3,1,2,5,4
(d) 5,2,1,3,4

Question 17: Identify the correct logic sequence.

1. Punishment
2. Prison
3. Arrest
4. Crime
5. Judgement

Options:

(a) 5,1,2,3,4
(b) 4,3,5,2,1
(c) 4,3,5,1,2
(d) 2,3,1,5,4

Answers

1. (a)	6. (d)	11. (c)	16. (b)
2. (c)	7. (b)	12. (b)	17. (c)
3. (b)	8. (c)	13. (d)	
4. (b)	9. (d)	14. (d)	
5. (c)	10. (b)	15. (c)	

Mathematical/Numerical Operations

Introduction:

Mathematical operation can be defined as simplification of expression containing numbers and different mathematical signs. There are four fundamental of mathematical operation such as, Addition ('+'), subtraction ('-'), division ('÷') and multiplication('x') and also statements such as less than ('<'), greater than('>'), equal to('='), not equal to ('≠'), notgreater than ('≯'), not less than(' ≮ ')etc., are also represented by symbols.

In these type of questions, an equation is represented by different symbols and signswhich may be different from the usual ones. The equation involves these operations are a set,using artificial symbols. In other words, the equation may also be used by giving a proper definition of the symbol used. Students are required to substitute the real signs in the place of artificial symbols to solve the questions.

In this type of questions, to find the value of given expression are must replace the symbol by mathematical operations. Then apply the BODMAS rule.

B – Bracket   O – Of   D –Division M – Multiplication

A – Addition S – Subtraction

Type I – Symbol Substitution

In this type of questions, students are provided with substitutes for various mathematical symbols, followed by question involving calculation of an expression or choosing the correct/incorrect equation. Students are required to put in the real signs in the given equation and solve the question as required.

EXAMPLE 1

If '+' means 'minus', '-' means 'multiply', '÷'means 'plus' and 'x' means divide, then 10 x 5 ÷ 3 -2 + 3 is equal to

(a) 5
(b) 53/3
(c) 21
(d) 36

Ans: (a)

Explanation: After using the correct symbols, we have $10 \div 5 + 3 \times 2 - 3 = 2 + 6 - 3 = 5$

Type II – Interchange of signs and numbers

In this type of questions, the given equation become correct and fully balanced, when either two signs of the equation or both the numbers and signs of the equation are interchanged. The candidate is required to find the correct paid of signs and numbers from the given alternatives.

EXAMPLE 2

If '+' and '-'signs are interchanged, similarly 'x' and '÷' signs are interchanged, then find the answer of the following equation.

10 – 2 +12 x 1 ÷ 0

(a) 8
(b) 12

(c) 1

(d) 0

Ans: (b)

Explanation: According to the question, after interchanging the signs 10 + 2 − 12 ÷ 1 x 0 = 10 + 2 − 12 x 0 = 10+2-0= 12.

EXAMPLE 3

Which interchanging of signs will make the following equation correct?

(16-4) x 6 ÷ 2 + 8 = 30

(a)   ÷ and −

(b) 4 and 2

(c) − and +

(d) 16 and 6

Ans: (a)

Explanation: The values after interchanging signs is

(16 ÷ 4) x 6 −2 + 8 = 30

4 x 6 − 2 + 8 = 30

24 + 6 = 30.

Exercise

Question 1:Fill the arithmetical operations in the blank places.

4 _ 3 _ 4 = 48

(a) xx
(b) ++
(c) x+
(d) +-

Question 2: Some equations are solved on the basis of a certain system. On the same basis find out the correct answer for the unsolved equation

1.   2 x 3 x 4 = 432
2.   5 x 6 x 7 = 765
3.   7 x 8 x 9 = 987
4.   2 x 5 x 7 = ?

Options:

(a) 572
(b) 752
(c) 725
(d) 257

Question 3: If 3 x 9 x 7 = 379, 5 x 4 x 8 = 584, then 1 x 2 x 3 = ?

(a) 123
(b) 231
(c) 213
(d) 132

Question 4:If 526 = 9 and 834 = 9, then 716 = ?

(a) 20
(b) 15

(c) 9

(d) 12

Question 5:If '-' means 'multiply', 'x' means 'plus', '+' means 'divide' and '÷' means 'minus', then 40 x 12 x 3 – 6 ÷ 60 = ?

(a) 44

(b) 16

(c) 7.95

(d) 4

Question 6: If 4x6x9=694, 5x3x2=325, then 7x8x2=?

(a) 729

(b) 872

(c) 827

(d) 279

Question 7: If 2463 = 36 and 5552 = 30, then 6732 = ?

(a) 32

(b) 36

(c) 34

(d) 39

Question 8:If x means -, + means ÷, - means x and ÷ means +, then 15 – 2 ÷ 900 + 90 x 100 is equal to

(a) 190

(b) 180

(c) 90

(d) -60

Question 9:If + means ÷ , ÷ means - , - means x , x means +, then12 + 6 ÷ 3 – 2 x 8 is equal to

(a) -1

(b) 2

(c) 4

(d) 8

Question 10: If x means ÷, - means x , ÷ means + and + means -, then (3 – 15 ÷ 19) x 8 + 6 is equal to

(a) -1

(b) 2

(c) 4

(d) 8

Question 11:If ÷ means x, x means +, + means -, and – means ÷, find the value of 16 x 3 + 5 – 2 ÷ 4

(a) 9

(b) 10

(c) 19

(d) 12

Question 12:If + means -, - means x , ÷ means + and x means ÷, then15 – 3 + 10 x 5 ÷ 5 is equal to

(a) 5

(b) 22

(c) 48

(d) 52

Question 13: If x means +, + means ÷, - means x, ÷ means -, then 8x 7 – 8 + 40 ÷ 2 is equal to

(a) 1

(b) 7.4

(c) 8.6

(d) 44

Question 14: If + means -, - means x, ÷ means + and x means ÷,
then 25 – 3 + 15 x 5 ÷ 5 is equal to

(a) 5
(b) 62
(c) 77
(d) 12

Question 15: If + means -, - means x , x means ÷, ÷ means +, then
40 ÷ 360 x 24 – 4 + 18 is equal to

(a) 118
(b) 82
(c) 72
(d) 90

Question 16:If $ means +, # means -, @ means x, and * means ÷,
then what is the value of 16 $ 4 @ 5 # 72 * 8 ?

(a) 25
(b) 27
(c) 29
(d) 36

Question 17:If + means ÷, - means +, x means -, and ÷ means x,
then what will be the value of [{(17 x 12) – (4 ÷2)} + (23-6)] ÷ 0.

(a) Infinite
(b) 0
(c) 118
(d) 219

Question 18:If Q means +, J means x, T means -, and K means ÷,
then 30 K 2 Q 3 J 6 T 5 is equal to

(a) 18
(b) 28

(c) 31
(d) 103

Question 19:If + means -, x means ÷, ÷ means +, and – means x, then what will be the value of 252 x 9 – 5 + 32 ÷92 ?

(a) 95
(b) 168
(c) 192
(d) 200

Question 20:If P means ÷, T means +, M means -, and D means x, then what is the value of 12 M 12 D 28 P 7 T 15?

(a) -30
(b) -15
(c) -21
(d) 45

Question 21:If P means x, R means +, T means ÷ and S means -, then 18 T 3 P 9 S 8 R 6 is equal to?

(a) -1.3333
(b) 0.6667
(c) 46
(d) 52

Question 22:If + stands for ÷, ÷ stands for x, x stands for -, - stands for +, then which one of the following is correct?

(a) 18 ÷ 6 x 7 + 5 – 2 = 22
(b) 18 x 6 + 7 ÷ 5 – 2 = 18
(c) 18 ÷ 16 – 7 + 5 x 2 = 20
(d) 18 + 6 ÷ 7 x 5 – 2 = 18

Question 23:If – means ÷, + means x, ÷ means -, x means +, then which of the following equation is correct?

(a) 52 ÷ 4 +5 x 8 – 2 = 36
(b) 43 x 7 ÷ 5 + 4 – 8 = 25
(c) 36 x 4 – 12 + 5 ÷ 3 = 420
(d) 36 – 12 x 6 ÷ 3 + 4 = 60

Question 24: If – means ÷, + means x, ÷ means – and x means +, then which one of the following equations is correct?

(a) 6 + 20 – 12 ÷ 7 – 1 = 38
(b) 6 – 20 ÷ 12 x 7 + 1 = 57
(c) 6 + 20 – 12 ÷ 7 x 1 = 62
(d) 6 ÷ 20 x 12 + 7 – 1 = 70

Question 25: if x means +, < means -, + means ÷, > means x, - means =, ÷ means >, = means <, then which of the following is true?

(a) 3 x 4 > 2 – 9 + 3 < 3
(b) 5 x 3 < 7 ÷ 8 + 4 x 1
(c) 5 > 2 + 2 = 10 < 4 x 8
(d) 3 x 2 < 4 ÷ 16 > 2 + 4

Question 26: Chose the appropriate combination of signs to solve the given equation.

(23-5) * (12÷2) * 3 * 16

(a) + + =
(b) - ÷ =
(c) X ÷ =
(d) + - =

Question 27:If P stands for -, Q stands for x , R stands for ÷, S stands for +, then what is the value of given equation?

14 Q 3 P 12 S 4 R 2 = ?

(a) 17
(b) 32
(c) 28
(d) 6

Question 28: If K means -, L means ÷, M means +, and D means x, then 117 L 3 K 5 M 12 D 8 = ?

(a) 150
(b) 125
(c) 130
(d) 145

Question 29:If 2 x 16 = 8; 8 x 8 = 1; 6 x 12 = 2, then 12 x 144 is equal to

(a) 16
(b) 24
(c) 11
(d) 12

Question 30: Some equations are solved on the basis of a certain system. Using the same, solve the unsolved equation.

If 10 – 3 = 12, 12 – 4 = 13, 14 – 5 = 14, then 16 – 6 = ?

(a) 16
(b) 18
(c) 10
(d) 15

Question 31:Let J = 1, K = 2, L = 5, M = 7, N = 11, O = 13, P = 17.
Find the letter to be inserted in the box in the equation given.

(N x ▢ + M) ÷ K = 31

(a) L
(b) P
(c) J
(d) O

Question 32:Select the correct combination of mathematical signs
to replace ' * ' signs and to balance the given equation.

24 * 34 * 2 * 5 * 12

(a) + ÷ x =
(b) = ÷ + -
(c) = ÷ - +
(d) + ÷ = x

Question 33:Select the correct combination of mathematical signs
to replace * signs and to balance the given equation.

5 * 6 * 5 * 8 * 14

(a) + - x =
(b) x ÷ + =
(c) ÷ x = -
(d) + x - ÷

Question 34: Which Sequence of mathematical symbols can
replace in the given equation?   8 * 5 * 9 * 31

(a) – x =
(b) - = x
(c) = x –
(d) x – =

Question 35: If 6 * 5 = 31, 7 * 8 = 57, 3 * 4 = 13, then 9 * 10 is equal to

(a) 90
(b) 91
(c) 81
(d) 10

Question 36: Select the correct combination of mathematical signs to replace * signs and to balance the given equation.

15 * 5 * 3 * 25

(a) = ÷ ×
(b) × ÷ =
(c) ÷ × =
(d) × = ÷

Question 37:Select the correct combination of mathematical signs to replace * signs and to balance the given equation.

96 * 6 * 8 * 2

(a) ÷ = ×
(b) × = +
(c) = ÷ ×
(d) = × ÷

Question 38:If $ means +, # means -, @ means x and * means ÷, then 1 6 $ 4 @ 5 # 7 2 * 8 is

(a) 25
(b) 27
(c) 29
(d) 36

Question 39: If 4 * 2 @ 3 = 6, 18 * 6 @ 4 = 12, then what will be the value of 24 * 3 @ 7 ?

(a) 21
(b) 27
(c) 72
(d) 56

Question 40:If P denotes x, T denotes - , M denotes +, and B denotes ÷, then 2 8 B 7 P 8 T 6 M 4 is equal to

(a) – 3/2
(b) 30
(c) 32
(d) 34

Question 41: If A for + , M for x, D for ÷, G for >, L for <, then which of the following Neill be logically correct?

(a) 4A 5D 3G 6A 2M 3
(b) 4A 5M 4L 6D 2A 8
(c) 4D 2A 4G 6D 2A 4
(d) 4A 3M 2L 4D 2M 6

Question 42:If P denotes x, T denotes - , M denotes +, and B denotes ÷, then 12 P 6 M 15 T 16 B 4 is equal to

(a) 70
(b) 83
(c) 75
(d) 110

Question 43:If P denotes ÷ , Q denotes x, R denotes + and S denotes -, then 18 Q 12 P 4 R 5 S 6 is equal to

(a) 95
(b) 53

(c) 51

(d) 57

Question 44:If R means ÷, Q means x, P means +, then 18 R 9 P 2 Q 8 is equal to

(a) 18

(b) 16

(c) 28

(d) 30

Question 45: If L stands for +, M stands for -, N stands for x, P stands for ÷, then 14 N 10 L 4 2 P 2 M 8 is equal to

(a) 153

(b) 216

(c) 248

(d) 25

Answers

1. (a)	12. (c)	23. (a)	34. (d)	45. (a)
2. (b)	13. (b)	24. (d)	35. (b)	
3. (d)	14. (c)	25. (c)	36. (b)	
4. (d)	15. (b)	26. (b)	37. (a)	
5. (d)	16. (b)	27. (b)	38. (b)	
6. (c)	17. (b)	28. (c)	39. (d)	
7. (a)	18. (b)	29. (d)	40. (b)	
8. (d)	19. (d)	30. (d)	41. (d)	
9. (c)	20. (c)	31. (a)	42. (b)	
10. (b)	21. (d)	32. (c)	43. (b)	
11. (a)	22. (d)	33. (b)	44. (a)	

Hints and Solutions

1. From the option (a), 4 x 3 x 4 = 48.

2. The 1st and 3rd number are interchanged in each equation, So by interchanging the 7 and 2, we get 752.

3. The 2nd and 3rd numbers are interchanged in each equation, whereas others remain constant. By interchanging the 3 and 2, we get 132.

4. 5-2+6= 9, 8-3+4= 9, Similarly 7-1+6=12

5. According to the equation, putting real values of signs,

$$40 + 12 \div 3 \times 6 - 60$$

$$= 40 + 4 \times 6 - 60$$

$$= 40 + 24 - 60 = 4$$

6. The 1st digit moved to 3rd place, 2nd one moved to 1st place and 3rd one moved to 2nd place. So we get 827.

7. As (2+4+6) x 3 = 12 x 3 = 36

And (5+5+5) x 2 = 30, similarly (6+7+3) x 2 = 32.

8. Using the correct symbols, we get,

$$15 \times 2 + 900 \div 90 - 100$$

$$15 \times 2 + 10 - 100 = 30 + 10 - 100 = -60$$

9. Using the correct symbols, we get

$$12 \quad 6 - 3 \times 2 + 8$$

$$= 2 - 3 \times 2 + 8 = 2 - 6 + 8 = 4$$

10. Using the correct symbols, we get,

$$(3 \times 15 + 19) \div 8 - 6$$

$$= (45 + 19) \div 8 - 6 = 64 \div 8 - 6 = 8 - 6 = 2$$

11. Using the correct symbols, we get,

$$16 + 3 - 5 \div 2 \times 4$$

$$= 16 + 3 - 2.5 \times 4 = 16 + 3 - 10 = 9$$

12. Using the correct symbols, we get,

$$15 \times 3 - 10 \div 5 + 5$$

$$= 15 \times 3 - 2 + 5 = 45 - 2 + 5 = 48$$

13. Using the correct symbols, we get,

$$= 8 + 7 \times 8 \div 40 - 2$$

$$= 8 + 7 \times 0.2 - 2 = 8 + 1.4 - 2 = 7.4$$

14. Using the correct symbols, we get,

$$25 \times 3 - 15 \div 5 + 5$$

$$= 25 \times 3 - 3 + 5 = 75 - 3 + 5 = 77$$

15. Using the correct symbols, we get,

$$40 + 360 \div 24 \times 4 - 18$$

$$= 40 + 15 \times 4 - 18 = 40 + 60 - 18 = 82$$

16. Using the correct symbols, we get,

$$16 + 4 \times 5 - 72 \div 8$$

$$= 16 + 4 \times 5 - 9 = 16 + 20 - 9 = 27$$

17. Using the correct symbols, we get,

$$[\{(17-12) + (4 \times 2)\} \div (23 + 6)] \times 0 = 0$$

18. Using the correct symbols, we get,

$$30 \div 2 + 3 \times 6 - 5$$

$$= 15 + 3 \times 6 - 5 = 15 + 18 - 5 = 28$$

19. Using the correct symbols, we get,

$$252 \div 9 \times 5 - 32 + 92$$

$$= 28 \times 5 - 32 + 92 = 140 - 32 + 92 = 200$$

20. Using the correct symbols, we get,

$$12 - 12 \times 28 \div 7 + 15$$

$$= 12 - 12 \times 4 + 15 = 12 - 48 + 15 = -21$$

21. Using the correct symbols, we get,

$$18 \div 3 \times 9 - 8 + 6$$

$$= 6 \times 9 - 8 + 6 = 54 - 8 + 6 = 52.$$

22. Using the correct symbols in (d) we get,

$$18 \div 6 \times 7 - 5 + 2$$

$$= 3 \times 7 - 5 + 2 = 21 - 5 + 2 = 18$$

23. Using the correct symbols in (a) we get,

$$52 - 4 \times 5 + 8 \div 2$$

$$= 52 - 4 \times 5 + 4 = 52 - 20 + 4 = 36$$

24. Using the correct symbols in (d) we get,

$$6 - 20 + 12 \times 7 \div 1$$

$$= 6 - 20 + 12 \times 7 = 6 - 20 + 84 = 70$$

25. Using the correct symbols in (c) we get,

$$5 \times 2 \div 2 < 10 - 4 + 8$$

$$5 \times 1 < 14 \text{ or } 5 < 14, \text{ which is true.}$$

26. Place signs in the question according to the option (b), we get
$(23-5) - (12 \div 2) \div 3 = 16$

$$18 - 6 \div 3 = 18 - 2 = 16$$

27. By using correct symbols in the equation we get,

14 x 3 – 12 + 4 ÷ 2

= 14 x 3 – 12 + 2 = 42 – 12 + 2 = 32

28. By using correct symbols in the equation, we get,

117 ÷ 3 – 5 + 12 x 8

= 39 – 5 + 12 x 8 = 39 – 5 + 96 = 130

29. 16 ÷ 2 = 8; 8 ÷ 8 = 1; 12 ÷ 6 = 2, Similarly

144 ÷ 12 = 12

30. As 10- 3 = 7, then 7 + 5 = 12

12 – 4 = 8, then 8 + 5 = 13, similarly

16 – 6 = 10, then 10 + 5 = 15.

31. According to the values given in the question,

(11 x ⬜ + 7) ÷ 2 = 31

11 x ⬜ + 7 = 62;

11 x ⬜ = 62 – 7;

11 x. ⬜ =55

⬜ = 55 ÷ 11 = 5

32. According to option (c), 24 = 34 ÷ 2 – 5 + 12

24 = 17 – 5 + 12 ; 24 = 24

33. From option (b) we get, 5 x 6 ÷ 5 + 8 = 14

5 x 1.2 + 8 = 14 ; 6 + 8 = 14 ; 14 = 14 , which is true.

34. From option (d) we get, 8 x 5 – 9 = 31

40 – 9 = 31; 31 = 31.

35. As 6 * 5 = 6 x 5 + 1 = 31;

    7*8 = 7 x 8 + 1 = 57;

    3*4 = 3 x 4 + 1 = 13;

    Similarly, 9*10= 9 x 10 + 1 = 91

36. From option (b), we get $15 \times 5 \div 3 = 25$

    $75 \div 3 = 25$; $25 = 25$.

37. From option (a), we get

    $96 \div 6 = 8 \times 2$; $16 = 16$.

38. Using the correct symbols, we have,

    $=16 + 4 \times 5 - 72 \div 8$

    $=16 + 4 \times 5 - 9 = 16 + 20 - 9 = 27$

39. Here sign * implies division and sign @ implies multiplication

    $4 \div 2 \times 3 = 6$; $18 \div 6 \times 4 = 12$

    Therefore, $24 \div 3 \times 7 = 56$

40. Using the proper symbols, we have

    $= 28 \div 7 \times 8 - 6 + 4$

    $= 4 \times 8 - 6 + 4 = 32 - 6 + 4 = 30$

41. Using the proper symbols in (d), we get

    $4 + 3 \times 2 < 4 \div 2 \times 6$

    $10 < 12$

42. Using the proper symbols, we get

    $=12 \times 6 + 15 - 16 \div 4$

    $=12 \times 6 + 15 - 4 = 72 + 15 - 4 = 83$

43. After assigning the signs to the alphabets,

we get 18 x 12 ÷ 4 + 5 – 6

= 18 x 3 + 5 – 6 = 54 + 5 – 6 = 53

44. Using the correct symbols, we get

= 18 ÷ 9 + 2 x 8

= 2 + 2 x 8 = 2 + 16 = 18.

45. Using the correct symbols, we get

= 14 x 10 + 42 ÷ 2 – 8

= 14 x 10 + 21 – 8 = 140 + 21 – 8 = 153.

Problem Solving

Introduction:

Problem solving is nothing more than general intelligence. Question asked from this chapter generally depends on mathematical rules and social intelligence.

To solve these types of questions, students must be aware about general intelligence and real mathematical operation.

Problem solving is a procedure to provide the best alternative solution on any difficulty.

EXAMPLE 1

There are twelve dozen of apple in a basket. Two dozen are added later. Ten apples got spoilt and are removed. The remaining are transferred equally into two baskets. How may apples are there in each basket?

(a) 89
(b) 168
(c) 158
(d) 79

Ans: (d)

Explanation:Initial number of apples in basket is 12 × 12= 144. Again, after two dozen of apples are added in the basket = 144 + (12 × 2) = 144 + 24 = 168. After 10 apples got spoilt and removed, remainingnumber of apples in basket is 168 – 10 = 158. So, after transferred equally into two baskets, number of apples in each basket = 158 ÷ 2 = 79.

EXAMPLE 2

Ali has $320. He spent 3/4th of it to buy a watch. Of the remainder, he used 1/8th of it to buy a pen. How much money is left?

(a) $ 120
(b) $ 90
(c) $ 70
(d) $ 100

Ans: (c)

Explanation: After purchasing the watch, remaining amount of Ali is   320 – 320 x ¾ = 320 – 240 = $ 80. After purchasing the pen, remaining amount of Ali is   80 – 80 x 1/8 = 80 – 10 = $ 70.

EXAMPLE 3

A family consisted of a man, his wife, his three sons, their wives and their three children in each son's family. How many members are there in the family?

(a) 12
(b) 13
(c) 15
(d) 17

Ans: (d)

Explanation: Total number of members of the family
=1+1+3+3+(3x3) = 8+9 = 17.

Exercise

Question 1: A library has an average of 510 visitors on Sunday and 240 visitors on other days. Then, the average number of visitors per day in a 30 days month beginning with a Sunday is

(a) 276
(b) 285
(c) 250
(d) 280

Question 2: A certain number of horses and equal number of men are going somewhere. All the men are walking along with their horses. If number of legs walking on ground is 90, how many horses are there?

(a) 15
(b) 25
(c) 16
(d) 5

Question 3: If you write all the numbers from 1 to 100, then how many times do you write 9?

(a) 11
(b) 18
(c) 20
(d) 21

Question 4: John saved $ 1000 in his bank account for a term of 6 months and earned an interest of 12% per annum. How much amount John earned as interest?

(a) $ 120
(b) $ 60
(c) $ 1120

(d) $1060

Question 5:Benjamin has 250 pens. From that he sold 150 pens, and 30 pens had been stolen. Represent the Sales volume in Percentage?

(a) 72 %
(b) 80 %
(c) 60 %
(d) 50 %

Question 6: The regular price of a toy is $ 2. If it's bought in multiples of 10, 10% of the price will be discounted. Then what is the total cost for buying 50 toys.

(a) 100
(b) 50
(c) 80
(d) 90

Question 7:An herd has 15 horses, 10 sheep's, and 5 hens. 2 of the hens are on tree. Count the number of legs on ground?

(a) 106
(b) 110
(c) 112
(d) 120

Answers

1. (b)	4. (b)	7. (a)
2. (a)	5. (c)	
3. (c)	6. (d)	

Hints and Solutions

1. We know that in a 30 days month beginning with a Sunday, there are 5 Sunday's and 25 other days.

     Average number of visitors on Sunday = 510

     Average number of visitors on other day = 240

     So, average number of visitors per day in a 30 days month = [(510 x 5) + (240 x 25)] ÷ 30 = 285.

2. Let the number of horses = number of men = 'y'. Horse has 4 legs and men have 2. In a pair of a horse and a man we get 6 legs. So, the number of pair is 6y=90. y = 90 ÷ 6 = 15. So, there are 15 horses and 15 men.

3. According to the Question, From 1 to 100, 9 as one digit 9,19,29,39,49,59,69,79,89,99

     9 as tens digit 90,91,92,93,94,95,96,97,98

     So, the total number of 9's from 1 to 100 is 20.

4. The interest specified in the problem is for a year. But John has invested for a term of 6 months, So, his interest would be 1000 x 12 % x 6 ÷ 12 = $ 60.

5. Percentage of sales = 150 ÷ 250 x 100 = 60 %.

     The stolen pens should not be treated as sales.

6. Price of the toy when bought in multiples of 10 is

     2 – (2 x 10%) = 2 – 0.2 = $ 1.8

     Cost of 50 toys = 50 x 1.8 = $ 90.

7. Horses and sheep's have 4 legs each. Hens has 2 legs each. So

$(15 \times 4) + (10 \times 4) + [(5 - 2) \times 2] = 60+40+6 = 106$.

Introduction:

In this types of questions, one or two combined set of letters and numbers are given. Each and every letter is coded by a number of two digits. Answer of these questions can be divided from the letters given in matrix on the basis of their related numbers. The code of an article can be classified by the combination of rows and columns. The instruction of of using rows and columns is given in the questions.

EXAMPLE 1

A word is represented by only one set of numbers as given in any one of the alternatives. The sets of numbers given in the alternative or represented by two classes of alphabets as in two matrices given below. The columns and rows of matrix I are number from 0 to 4 and that of matrix II are number from 5 to 9. A letter from these matrices can be represented first by its row and next by its column. E.g., 'A' can be represented by 55, 67 etc., and 'R' can be represented by 23,30 etc. Similarly, identify

the set for the word DART.

Matrix I

	0	1	2	3	4
0	F	O	M	S	R
1	S	R	F	O	M
2	O	M	S	R	F
3	R	F	O	M	S
4	M	S	R	F	O

Matrix II

	5	6	7	8	9
5	A	T	D	I	P
6	I	P	A	T	D
7	T	D	I	P	A
8	P	A	T	D	I
9	D	I	P	A	T

Options:

(a) 69,67,11,86
(b) 76,86,03,87
(c) 57,55,04,56
(d) 95,98,42,65

Ans: (c)

Explanation: D = 57,69,76,88,95 ; A = 55,67,79,86,98 ; R=04,11,23,30,42, T = 56,68,75,87,99. Therefore DART=57,55,04,56.

EXAMPLE 2:

A word is represented by only one set of numbers as given in any one of the alternatives. The sets of numbers given in the alternative or represented by two classes of alphabets as in two matrices given below. The columns and rows of matrix I are number from 0 to 4 and that of matrix II are number from 5 to 9. A letter from these matrices can be represented first by its row and next by its column. E.g., M can be represented by 01,10 etc., and R can be represented by 58,85 etc. Similarly, you have to identify the set for the word 'NOW'.

Matrix I   ### Matrix II

	0	1	2	3	4
0	I	M	W	S	Q
1	M	W	S	Q	I
2	W	S	Q	I	M
3	S	Q	I	M	W
4	Q	I	M	W	S

	5	6	7	8	9
5	O	A	D	R	N
6	A	D	R	N	O
7	D	R	N	O	A
8	R	N	O	A	D
9	N	O	A	D	R

Options:

(a) 55,78,11
(b) 86,58,11
(c) 95,55,34
(d) 95,67,02

Ans: (c)

Explanation: From option (c), N = 95 ; O = 55 ; W = 34.

Exercise

Question 1:From the matrices given below identify the set for the word ' BEE'

Matrix I

	0	1	2	3	4
0	F	A	N	O	I
1	I	O	F	A	N
2	A	N	O	I	F
3	O	F	I	N	A
4	N	I	A	F	O

Matrix II

	5	6	7	8	9
5	S	E	H	B	T
6	H	S	E	T	B
7	B	T	S	E	H
8	E	H	T	B	S
9	T	S	E	H	B

Options:

(a) 12,25,33
(b) 21,12,22
(c) 12,15,41
(d) 12,21,15

Question 2: From the matrices given below identify the setfor the word ' FAITH'

Matrix I

	0	1	2	3	4	5
0	A	B	C	D	D	E
1	E	D	A	B	B	C
2	B	C	D	E	E	A
3	D	A	E	C	C	D
4	C	E	B	A	A	B

Matrix II

	6	7	8	9	10
6	F	G	H	I	J
7	J	I	G	H	F
8	F	H	I	J	G
9	G	J	F	G	I
10	H	E	J	F	E

(a) 24,31,10,59,57

(b) 12,20,40,68,65

(c) 31,34,23,76,79

(d) 43,42,41,78,89

Question: Identify the correct set for eachword given in each question using the below matrices.

Matrix I

	0	1	2	3	4
0	D	O	B	A	I
1	O	B	A	I	D
2	B	A	I	D	O
3	A	I	D	O	B
4	I	D	O	B	A

Matrix II

	5	6	7	8	9
5	W	N	R	M	L
6	N	R	M	L	W
7	R	M	L	W	N
8	M	L	W	N	R
9	L	W	N	R	M

3. DOWN

(a) 41,66,23,55

(b) 82,75,44,76

(c) 32,24,87,88

(d) 14,89,12,78

4. BOND

(a) 43,21,97,33

(b) 11,33,79,41

(c) 34,44,66,14

(d) 20,30,89,23

5.BOLD

(a) 11,68,42,69

(b) 21,95,33,97

(c) 34,24,59,14

(d) 34,86,44,78

6.RAIN

(a) 57,12,31,56

(b) 57,21,23,79

(c) 66,44,42,96

(d) 75,30,31,87

7.LAND

(a) 68,21,79,41

(b) 77,44,76,33

(c) 86,21,67,12

(d) 95,30,80,20

Question: Identify the correct set for the each word given in each question using the below matrices.

Matrix I   **Matrix II**

	0	1	2	3	4
0	A	E	S	T	H
1	T	H	A	E	S
2	E	S	T	H	A
3	H	A	E	S	T
4	S	T	H	A	E

	5	6	7	8	9
5	P	O	R	K	L
6	K	L	P	O	R
7	O	R	K	L	P
8	L	P	O	R	K
9	R	K	L	P	O

8. TASTE
(a)   44,32,21,03,33
(b)   32,31,02,04,12
(c)   34,00,40,22,44
(d)   13,12,14,10,76

9. HORSE
(a) 95,75,02,32,59
(b) 04,75,88,21,32
(c) 86,67,33,44,13
(d) 57,87,32,33,24

10. SOLO
(a) 41,57,87,31
(b) 33,99,66,75
(c) 21,75,44,02
(d) 02,78,87,13

11. LAKE
(a) 97,00,77,12
(b) 66,12,58,40
(c) 85,31,77,44
(d) 77,43,76,31

12. LEAST
(a) 97,32,31,34,10
(b) 87,32,2131,44
(c) 85,01,00,40,41

(d) 66,00,20,34,33

Question: Identify the correct set for the each word given in each question using the below matrices.

	0	1	2	3	4	5	6	7	8	9	10
0	H	A	Z	N	X	P	Y	K	A	D	X
1	C	G	P	H	S	G	B	G	E	V	A
2	N	S	C	V	B	W	U	W	L	K	Z
3	Z	W	M	G	E	S	B	K	D	M	B
4	Q	A	Y	O	Y	P	J	A	H	V	R
5	A	K	E	C	U	J	V	S	B	R	Y
6	D	X	A	W	G	H	Q	Z	X	A	D
7	X	L	F	I	Q	V	B	E	S	J	R
8	V	D	O	U	H	S	G	W	Z	D	S
9	U	N	T	L	V	A	D	U	R	B	Z
10	S	B	G	W	Q	I	E	A	Y	O	B

13. LOVELY
(a) 39,34,93,28,21,49
(b) 39,34,57,610,82,60
(c) 82,91,28,25,48,76
(d) 17,28,65,49,65,43

14. PASSION
(a) 54,10,75,73,43,19,02
(b) 21,14,87,12,37,82,19
(c) 54,59,41,810,73,28,02
(d) 50,96,108,58,37,34,30

15. BUS STOP
(a) 34, 87,65,95,68,12,09
(b) 67,45,58,87,29,34,50
(c) 40,49,38,72,16,45,63
(d) 11,71,68,98,46,37,41

16. HONEST
(a) 53,76,93,84,61,12
(b) 21,42,63,48,96,05
(c) 48,28,02,81,87,29
(d) 12,24,63,84,06,27

17. UNITED
(a) 38,19,37,29,25,69
(b) 09,81,27,63,54,45
(c) 18,63,45,15,49,69
(d) 21,99,105,88,02,90

Question 18:   Identify the correct set for the word TEMPT using the below matrices.

Matrix I

	0	1	2	3	4
0	A	U	O	T	B
1	T	E	P	A	W
2	R	M	G	G	I
3	U	M	M	C	L
4	P	L	N	E	C

Matrix II

	5	6	7	8	9
5	P	T	A	M	E
6	G	I	O	T	M
7	E	A	L	T	M
8	R	A	B	L	T
9	N	P	E	G	P

(a) 56,43,32,97,10
(b) 89,43,40,12,44
(c) 10,75,32,96,78
(d) 78,11,12,96,10

Answers

1. (d)	7. (a)	13. (b)
2. (c)	8. (c)	14. (d)
3. (c)	9. (b)	15. (b)
4. (b)	10. (b)	16. (c)
5. (c)	11. (c)	17. (a)
6. (a)	12. (c)	18. (c)

Arrangement and Rearrangements

Introduction:

In this a sequence of alphabets, numbers and symbols will be given in a shuffled manner. From that students are sometimes asked to arrange that sequence in ascending or descending order or may be asked to identify the effect on happening or non-happening of conditions given.

EXAMPLE 1

Study the following arrangement carefully and answer the questions given below:

BↃAM3#D2EK9$F@NIT41UW©H8%VJ5Y6*7R

1. How many such symbols are there in a above arrangements each of which is either immediately preceded by a letter or immediately followed by a letter but not both
(a) None
(b) One
(c) Two
(d) Three

Ans: (d)

Explanation: As 3#D, 9$F and 8%V are as above condition.

2. If all the symbols in the above arrangement are removed which of the following will be the twelfth from the left end?
(a) 9
(b) U
(c) I

(d) 1

Ans: (c)

Explanation: Without the symbols, the arrangement is

B A M 3 D 2 E K 9 F N (I) T 4 U W H 8 V J 5 Y 6 7 R

Exercise

Directions (Questions.1-4):

Study the following arrangement carefully and answer the questions given below:

B ↑ AM3#D2EK9$F@NIT41UW©H8%VJ5Y6*7R

1. How many such numbers are there in the above arrangement each of which is ok immediately followed by a consonant but not immediately proceeded by a letter?
(a) None
(b) One
(c) Two
(d) Three

2. Four of the following five are alike in a certain way based on their positions in the above arrangement and so form a group. Which is the one that does not belong to that group?
a) DK3
b) 4NU
c) 8JC
d) 5*%

3. Which of the following is the seventh to the right of the eighteenth from the right end of the above arrangement?
a) H
b) 9
c) %
d) E

4. How many such 7s are there in the following number sequence each of which is immediately proceeded by 5 and not immediately followed by 8?

2 3 5 7 8 9 3 4 5 7 6 1 9 3 5 7 4 8 3 2 5 7 8 8 9 2 5

(a) None
(b) One
(c) Two
(d) Three

Directions(Questions. 5-10):

Study the following arrangement carefully and answer the questions given below:

M4ET%J9IB@U8©N#WF1V7*2AH3Y5$6K

5. Which of the following is the nineth to the right of the seventeenth from the right end of the above arrangement
(a) A
(b) %
(c) I
(d) Y

6. What should come in the place of question mark(?) in the following series based on the above arrangement?

4T%9B@8N#FV7?

(a) 2H3
(b) 2HY
(c) *AH

(d) *A3

7. Four of the following five are alike in a certain way based on the above arrangement and so form a group. Which is the one that does not belong to the group?
(a) JIT
(b) 35A
(c) $KY
(d) 8©@

8. How many such vowels are there in the above arrangement each of which is immediately preceded by a number and immediately followed by a consonant?
(a) None
(b) One
(c) Two
(d) Three

9. How many such numbers are there in the above arrangement each of which is immediately followed by a symbol and immediately preceded by a consonant.
(a) None
(b) One
(c) Two
(d) Three

10. How many such symbols are there in the above arrangement each of which is immediately preceded by a consonant and not immediately followed by a consonant
(a) None
(b) One
(c) Two
(d) Three

Directions (Questions.11-15):

These questions are based on the following letter/number/symbol arrangement. Study it carefully and answer the questions.

7D5#AB1%K$4EJF3*2HI@L6QU©9MT8W

11. How many such symbols are there in the above arrangement each of which is immediately preceded by a vowel and also immediately followed by a number?
(a) None
(b) One
(c) Two
(d) Three

12. Four of the following five are alike in a certain way on the basis of their positions in the above arrangement and so form a group. Which is the one that does not belong to the group?
(a) K41
(b) *HF
(c) #B5
(d) M8©

13. Which of the following pairs of elements does not have the second element, immediately followed by the first element?
(a) 5#
(b) MT
(c) $4
(d) 3F

14. How many such numbers are in the above arrangement, each of which is immediately followed by the symbol and also immediately preceded by a consonant?
(a) None
(b) One
(c) Two
(d) Three

15. What will come in the place of question mark (?) in the series based on the above arrangement?

A # D $ K 1 3 F E?

(a) @12
(b) *HI
(c) H2@
(d) HIL

Directions (Questions. 16-22):

Study the following arrangement carefully and answer the question given below:

B#AR58E%MF4J1U@H2©9TI6*W3P#K7$Y

16. Which of the following is the twelfth to the left of twentieth from the left end of the above arrangement?
(a) %
(b) W
(c) $
(d) J

17. How many such numbers are there in the arrangement each of which is immediately preceded by a consonant and also immediately followed by a symbol?
(a) None
(b) One
(c) Two
(d) Three

18. How many such symbols are there in the above arrangement each of which is immediately preceded by a letter and also immediately followed by a number?
(a) None
(b) One
(c) Two
(d) Three

19. How many such consonants are there in the above arrangement each of which is immediately preceded by a consonant and also immediately followed by a number?
(a) None
(b) One
(c) Two
(d) Three

20. If all the numbers in the above arrangement are dropped which of the following will be the eleventh from the right end?
(a) U
(b) T
(c) F
(d) H

21. How many such vowels are there in the above arrangement each of which is either immediately preceded by a symbol or immediately followed by a symbol or both?
(a) None
(b) One
(c) Two
(d) Three

22. Four of the following are alike in a certain way based on their positions in the above arrangement and so form a groupwhich is the one that does not belong to that group?
(a) 1@4
(b) ©TH
(c) WP6

(d) 92I

Directions (Questions.23-25):

Following questions are based on the five three digits numbers given below:

518   725   849   387   634

23. If the positions of the first and third digits in each of the numbers are interchanged, which of the following will be the lowest number after rearrangement?
(a) 518
(b) 725
(c) 849
(d) 634

24. If the positions of the first and the second digits in each of the numbers are interchanged which of the following will be the third term from the top when they are arranged in descending order after the rearrangement?
(a) 518
(b) 725
(c) 634
(d) 849

25. If the positions of the second and the third digits in each number are interchanged. Which following will be the difference between highest and lowest number after the rearrangement
(a) 506
(b) 526

(c) 416

(d) 516

26. If the letters in the word COMPARE are rearranged in such a way that first the vowels within the word are rearranged alphabetically followed by the consonants arranged alphabetically, which of the following will be the fifth letter from the right end after the rearrangement?

(a) O

(b) E

(c) M

(d) P

27. If every alternate letter in the word SOLITARY starting from the first letter is replaced by the previous letter in the English alphabet and each of the remaining letters is replaced by the next letter in the English alphabet, which of the following will be the third letter from the right end after the Substitution?

(a) B

(b) S

(c) Z

(d) K

28. The positions of the first and the fifth digits in the number 84329517 are interchanged. Similarly, the positions of the second and the sixth digits are interchanged and so on. Which of the following will be the second from the right end after the rearrangement?

(a) 3

(b) 4

(c) 2

(d) 9

Directions (Questions.29-35):

Study the following arrangement carefully and answer the question given below:

MJ%4TEKI9#PA$Q38N5U7W*B@DF©1Z6H

29. How many such symbols are there in the above arrangement each of which is immediately preceded by a number and immediately followed by a consonant?
(a) None
(b) One
(c) Two
(d) Three

30. How many such consonants are there in the above arrangement, each of which is immediately preceded by a number and also immediately followed by a number?
(a) None
(b) One
(c) Two
(d) Three

31. If all the symbols are removed from the above arrangements, which of the following will be the sixth to the right of the thirteen from the right end?

(a) B

(b) 9

(c) D

(d) I

32. If all the numbers are removed from the above arrangement which of the following will be the fourth to the left of the twentieth from the left end?

(a) H

(b) 4

(c) B

(d) *

33. Four of the following five are alike in a certain way based on their positions in the above arrangement and so form a group. Which is the one that does not belong to that group?

(a) I9E

(b) 7W5

(c) ©1D

(d) QA3

34. What should come in place of the question mark(?) in the following series based on the above arrangement?

      J 4 E I # A Q 8 5 7 * @ ?

(a) F16
(b) D©Z
(c) F©6
(d) FIZ

35. Which of the following is exactly midway between K and W in the above arrangement?
(a) $
(b) 3
(c) 8
(d) None of these

Directions (Questions. 36-40):

These questions are based on the following arrangement:

D 5 4 I H π $K E 3 L B @ A R M 1 6 F % J € 2 7 C G 9

36. If all the digits are dropped from the above arrangement which of the following will be the fourth to the left of the seventh from the right end?
(a) B
(b) @
(c) L
(d) A

37. How many such symbols are there in the above arrangement each of which is either immediately followed or immediately preceded by a consonant but not both?
(a) One
(b) Two
(c) Three
(d) More than three

38. If the position of ten elements from the right end is reversed which of the following will be the fifth to the right of the thirteenth from the right?
(a) %
(b) F
(c) C
(d) G

39. How many such consonants are there in the above arrangement each of which is immediately proceeded by a vowel and also immediately followed by another consonant?
(a) None
(b) One
(c) Two
(d) Three

40. Four of the following five are alike in a certain way on the basis of their position in the above arrangement and so form a group. Which is the one that does not belong to the group?
(a) KL3
(b) F€J

(c) R61
(d) @MA

41. The positions of the first and the fifth digits in the number 94861723 are interchanged. Similarly, the positions of the second and the sixth digits are interchanged and so on. Which of the following will be the third digit from the right end after the rearrangement?
(a) 4
(b) 8
(c) 7
(d) 1

42. The consonants in the word CREATION first arranged alphabetically followed by the vowels arranged alphabetically. Which of the following will be the third letter to the right of the sixth letter from the right end?
(a) T
(b) I
(c) E
(d) O

Directions (Questions. 43-50):

Study the following arrangement carefully and answer the questions given below:

R P A 5 N % T 7 B 4 # J E $ M 2 1 D * I 8 H 3 U @ 9 F W 6 © K

43. How many such consonants are there in the above arrangement each of which is immediately followed by a vowel but not immediately preceded by a number?
(a) None
(b) One
(c) Two
(d) Three

44. How many such consonants are there in the above arrangement each of which is either immediately preceded by a vowel or immediately followed by a symbol but not both?
(a) One
(b) Two
(c) Three
(d) More than three

45. Four of the following five are alike in a certain way based on their positions in the above arrangement and so form a group. Which is the one that does not belong to that group?
(a) M1$
(b) WF©
(c) U93
(d) DI1

46. Which of the following is exactly between 4 and I in the above arrangement?
(a) M
(b) $
(c) 2
(d) 1

47. How many such symbols are there in the above arrangement each of which is not immediately followed by a number and immediately preceded by a consonant?
(a) None
(b) One
(c) Two
(d) Three

48. Which of the following is the fourth to the right of the seventeenth from the right end in the above arrangement?
(a) #
(b) *
(c) D
(d) J

49. What should come in place of the question mark (?) in the following series based on the above arrangement?

       A%7 4EM 1IH ?

(a) UF6
(b) U9W
(c) UF©

(d) 39W

50. Which of the following is the seventh to the left of the fifteenth from the left end in the above arrangement?
(a) H
(b) B
(c) I
(d) 7

Answers

1. (b)	11. (b)	21. (d)	31. (a)	41. (a)
2. (d)	12. (c)	22. (d)	32. (d)	42. (c)
3. (a)	13. (d)	23. (d)	33. (d)	43. (c)
4. (c)	14. (d)	24. (c)	34. (a)	44. (b)
5. (a)	15. (a)	25. (d)	35. (d)	45. (b)
6. (a)	16. (a)	26. (a)	36. (a)	46. (a)
7. (d)	17. (c)	27. (a)	37. (d)	47. (c)
8. (d)	18. (a)	28. (a)	38. (c)	48. (b)
9. (c)	19. (b)	29. (b)	39. (b)	49. (a)
10. (b)	20. (d)	30. (c)	40. (d)	50. (d)

Hints and solutions

1. Required arrangement is

    NOT LETTER – NUMBER – CONSONANT

    There is only such combination - *7R

2. D ——— K̶ ——— 3̶→

        +3   −5

      4 ———→N ———→ U

        +3   −5

      8 ———→J ———→C

        +3   −5

      F ———→K ———→N

        +3   −5

      5 ———→* ———→%

        +3   −6

3.

                    18th from the right end

B ↑A M 3 # D 2 E K 9 $ F @ N I T 4 1 U W © H 8 % V J 5 Y 6 * 7 R

                  7th from the right of I

4. Required arrangement is 5 7 not 8. Such arrangements in the given sequence are 576, 574.

5. 9th to the right of 17th from right end = 17 – 9

    = 8th from right end = A

6. Split the code into 6 sets containing 5 letters each. Consider the 2ⁿᵈ, 4ᵗʰ and 5ᵗʰ letters to form the sub code.

7. All the 1ˢᵗ letter of the option is succeeded by 2 letters and preceded by two letters except option (d).

8. Required arrangement is

NUMBER – VOWEL – CONSONANT

Such arrangements are 4ET, 9IB, 2AH.

9. Required arrangement is

CONSONANT – NUMBER – SYMBOL

Such arrangements are V7* and Y5$

10. Required arrangement is

CONSONANT – SYMBOL – NOT CONSONANT

Such combination is B@U

11. Required arrangement is

VOWEL – SYMBOL – NUMBER

Such arrangement is U©9

12. All the 1ˢᵗ letter of the option is succeeded by 2 letters and preceded by two letters except option (c).

13. 3F does not have the second element, immediately followed by the first element.

14. Required arrangement is CONSONANT-NUMBER-SYMBOL. Such arrangements are D5#, B1%, F3*.

15. Split the code into 6 sets containing 5 letters each. Consider the 5th, 4th and 2nd letters as in order to form the sub code.

16. 20th from the left end is T and 12th to the left of T is %.

17. Required arrangement is CONSONANT-NUMBER-SYMBOL. Such arrangements are H2© and K7$

18. Required arrangement is CONSONANT-NUMBER-SYMBOL. No such combination exists.

19. Required arrangement is CONSONANT-CONSONANT-NUMBER-. Such arrangements is MF4.

20. If all the numbers are removed then the arrangement will be B # A R E % M F J U @ H © T I * W P # K $ Y.

   11th from right end is H.

21. Required combinations: #A, E% and U@

22. All the 1st letter of the option is succeeded by 2 letters and preceded by two letters except option (d).

23. Number :   518   725   849   387   634

   Rearrangement: 815   527   948   783   436

   So, 634 is the lowest in the rearrangement.

24. Number :   518   725   849   387   634

   Rearrangement: 158   275   489   837   364

   Descending order:837   489   364   275   158

So, the third from top = 364 and the corresponding number is 634.

25. Number :   518   725   849   387   634

    Rearrangement: 581   752   894   378   643

Difference between the highest and lowest is

894 – 378 = 516

26. Rearrangement = AEOCMPR

Fifth letter from the right end = O.

27. S

Third from right end = B.

28. Rearrangement = 95178432

Second digit from the right end is 3.

29. Required combination is NUMBER-SYMBOLS-CONSONANT

Such combination is 9#P.

30. Required combination is NUMBER-CONSONANT-NUMBER

Such combination are 8N5 and Z6H .

31. Rearrangement without symbol:

M J 4 T E K I 9 P A Q 3 8 N 5 U 7 W B D F 1 Z 6 H

6th to the right of the 13th from the right end = 13 – 6 =

7th from the right end = B

32. MJ%TEKI#PA$QNUW*B@DF©ZH

    4th to the left of the 12th from the left end = 20 – 4

    = 16th from the left end = *

33. All the 1st letter of the option is succeeded by 1 letter and preceded by two letters except option (d).

34. All the letters in the even number places are rearranged. So the answer is F16.

35. Midway between K and W is Q.

36. Arrangement without digits.

$$D\ I\ H\ \pi\ \$K\ E\ L\ B\ @\ A\ R\ M\ F\ \%\ J\ €\ C\ G$$

4th to the left	7th from the right end

37. There are four such symbols Hπ, $K, B@, J£.

38.

13th from right

$$D\ 5\ 4\ I\ H\ \pi\ \$K\ E\ 3\ L\ B\ @\ A\ R\ M\ 1\ 9\ G\ C\ 7\ 2\ £\ J\ \%\ F\ 6$$

5th to the right

39. There is only one such arrangement – ARM

40. In others, 2nd and 3rd elements of a group occupy adjacent positions in the series.

41. Rearrangement : 1 7 2 3 9 4 8 6

    Third digit from the right end in the rearrangement is 4.

42. Word :   C R E A T I O N

    Rearrangement : C N T R A E I O

    Third letter of the right of the sixth letter from the right end
    = E

43. Required combination

    NOT NUMBER – CONSONANT – VOWEL

    Such combinations in the arrangement are RPA and #JE.

44. Required combination

    N% and D*

45. All the 1st letter of the option is succeeded by 2 letters and preceded by two letters except option (b).

46. 4   #   J   E $ (M) 2   1   D   *   1

    M is between 4 and I.

47. Required combination is

    CONSONANT – SYMBOL – NOT NUMBER

    Such combinations are N%T and D*I

48. 4th to the right of the 17th from right end = 17 – 4

    = 13th from the right end = *

49. The answer is UF6.

50. 7th to the left of the 15th from the left end = 15 -7

= 8th from the left end   = 7.

Analytical Reasoning

Introduction:

Analytical reasoning focuses on identifying the relationships and understanding the sequence between the given data. It helps the students in concentrating and understanding thinks better.

EXAMPLE 1

Eight friends Smith, Roger, Angel, Nick, Rachel, Jack, Mary and Amelia are sitting around a circular table facing the centre. Smith is second to the right of Amelia, but is not a neighbour of Angel. Nick is third to the left of Angel but is not next to Smith. Jack is second to the right of Rachel and third to the left of Mary.

As given in the question we first draw an arrangement as given as follows.

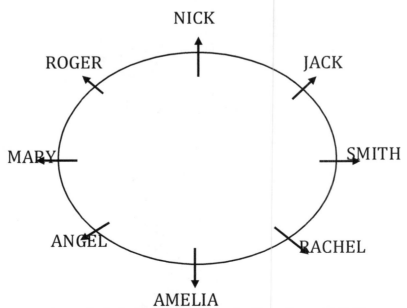

The above diagram helps to understand each ones position and answering the following questions

1. Who is second to the left of Amelia?
(a) Roger
(b) Rachel
(c) Angel
(d) Mary

Ans: (d)

2. Who is immediate to the right of Nick?
(a) Jack
(b) Roger
(c) Mary
(d) Jack or Roger

Ans: (b)

3. Which of the following is correct position of Rachel?
(a) To the immediate right of Amelia
(b) To the immediate left of Amelia
(c) To the immediate right of Smith
(d) Next to Jack.

Ans: (a)

4. Which of the following pairs represents the immediate neighbours of Nick?
(a) Jack and Mary
(b) Roger and Mary
(c) Smith and Jack
(d) Roger and Jack

Ans: (d)

5. Who is the immediate left of Smith?
(a) Jack
(b) Amelia
(c) Rachel
(d) Mary

Ans: (c)

Exercise

Study the following information carefully and answer the questions given below:

P, Q, R, T, S, T, V, and W are seven friends working in a call center. Each of them has different days off in a week from Monday to Sunday not necessarily in the same order. They work in three different shifts I, II, III with at least twoof them each shift.

R works in shift II and his day off is not Sunday. P's day off is Tuesday and he does not work in the same shift with either Q or W. None of these who work in shift I has day off either on Wednesday or on Friday. V works with only T in shift III. S's day off is Sunday, V's day off is immediate next day of that of R's day off. T's day off is not on Wednesday. W's day off is not on the previous day of P's day off. S works in shift I. Q does not work in the same shift with R and his day off is not on Thursday.

1.   Which of the following is W's day off?
(a) Tuesday
(b) Monday
(c) Saturday
(d) None of these

2.   Which of the following is R's day off?
(a) Friday
(b) Thursday
(c) Tuesday
(d) Wednesday

3. Which of the following group of friends work in shift III?
(a) RP
(b) RV
(c) QWS
(d) None of these

4. Which of the following is Q's day off?
(a) Friday
(b) Wednesday
(c) Thursday
(d) Monday

5. Which of the group of friends work in shift I ?
(a) RV
(b) RP
(c) QWS
(d) None of these

Study the following information carefully and answer the questions given below:

Seven professionals A, B, C, D, E, F, and G are practicing their professions in different cities Sydney, Perth, Brisbane, Melbourne, Adelaide, Hobart and Canberra not necessarily in the same order. Each has a different profession Doctor, Engineer, Pharmacist, Lawyer, Counsellor, Professor and Artist not necessarily in the same order. A is a Pharmacist and practices in Canberra, D practices in Perth but is not a Doctor or an Artist. The one who practices in Brisbane is a Professor. G is a counsellor and does not practice in Melbourne or Sydney. E is Lawyer and practices in

Adelaide. F practices in Sydney but is not an artist. C practices in Melbourne.

6. What is D's profession?
(a) Doctor
(b) Professor
(c) Engineer
(d) None of these

7. Who is the professor?
(a) B
(b) C
(c) D
(d) E

8. Which of the following combinations of profession and place is correct?
(a) Pharmacist – Hobart
(b) Engineer – Sydney
(c) Doctor – Perth
(d) Artist – Melbourne

9. Which of the following persons work in Hobart?
(a) B
(b) G
(c) C
(d) B or G

10. Who is the Doctor?

(a) D

(b) C

(c) B

(d) None of these.

Study the following information carefully and answer the questions given below:

M, N, P, R, T, W, F and H are sitting around a circle facing at the center. P is third to the left of M and second to the right of T. N is second to the right of P. R is second to the right of W is the second to the right of M. F is not an immediate neighbor of P.

11. Who is to the immediate right of P?

(a) H

(b) F

(c) R

(d) None of these

12. Who is the immediate right of H?

(a) R

(b) F

(c) M

(d) None of these

13. Who is the immediate left of R?

(a) P

(b) H

(c) W

(d) T

14. Who is the third to the right of R?
(a) T
(b) W
(c) R
(d) F

15. Who is second to right of F?
(a) M
(b) R
(c) T
(d) None of these

16. Which of the following is the first person sitting in between the second and third person?
(a) NHM
(b) PHN
(c) TRP
(d) TWF

Study the following information carefully and answer the questions given below:

P, Q, R, S, T,V and J are sitting around a circle facing the center. S is not immediate neighbor of V. S is the second on the right of T who is second to the right of Q. R is third of J and second to the left of P.

17. Who is the immediate right of Q?
(a) S
(b) R
(c) V
(d) None of these

18. What is the J's position with respect to P?
(a) Third to the Right
(b) Second to the left
(c) Second to the right
(d) None of these

19. How many of them are Q and S ?
(a) 2.only
(b) 3 only
(c) 4 only
(d) 2 or 3 only

20. Who among the following sitting between V and R ?
(a) Q
(b) J
(c) T
(d) S

Study the following information carefully and answer the questions given below:

   i.   A, B, C, D, E,F, G and H are sitting along a circular table facing the centre.
   ii.   D is neighbour of A but not of H.

iii.   B is neighbour of F and 4th the left of D.

iv.   E is neighbour of H and 3rd to the right of F.

v.   C is neither neighbour of A nor of G.

21. Which of the following is correct?

(a) D is to the immediate left of G

(b) A is between G and D

(c) F is 4th to the right of D

(d) E is between H and B

22. Which of the following is wrong?

(a) B is to the immediate left of H

(b) H is to the immediate left of E

(c) D is the 4th to the right of F

(d) C is the 4th to the left of F

23. Which of the following groups has the second person sitting in between the first and third?

(a) AFC

(b) GAD

(c) BEH

(d) HFB

24. Which of the following pairs has the second person sitting to the immediate left of the first?

(a) BH

(b) FB

(c) EG

(d) AD

25. Which of the following pairs has three persons sitting between them?
(a) CE
(b) FH
(c) DC
(d) ED

26. If C and G interchange their positions which of the following will indicate A's position?
(a) To immediate right of G
(b) 4th to the right of C
(c) 2nd to the left of G
(d) None of these

Study the following information carefully and answer the questions given below:

Eight persons A, B, C, D, E, F, G and H are sitting around a rectangular table in such a way that the two persons sit on each of four sides of the table facing the center. Persons sitting on opposite sides are exactly opposite to each other.

D faces north and sits exactly opposite to H. E is to the immediate left of H. A and G sit on the same side. G is exactly opposite of B who is to the immediate right of C. A is next to the left of D.

27. Who is sitting opposite to A?
(a) G

(b) D

(c) E

(d) None of these

28. Who is next to E in Clockwise direction?

(a) G

(b) B

(c) F

(d) A or F

29. Which of the following pair of persons has both the persons sitting on the same side with the first person sitting to the right of second person?

(a) DF

(b) CB

(c) FC

(d) AG

30. Who is sitting opposite to E?

(a) D

(b) A

(c) F

(d) A or D

31. Which of the following statement is definitely true?

(a) A is facing North

(b) E is sitting opposite of F

(c) F is to the left of G

(d) C is to the left of A

Answers

Question (1 -5)

Person	Off day	Shift
P	Tuesday	II
Q	Monday	I
R	Wednesday	II
S	Sunday	I
T	Friday	III
V	Thursday	III
W	Saturday	I

1. (c), W's day off is Saturday.
2. (d), R's day off is Wednesday.
3. (a), R and P work in shift II.
4. (d), Q's day off is Monday.
5. (c), QSW work in shift I.

Question (6-10)

Name	Profession	Cities
A	Pharmacist	Canberra
B	Professor	Brisbane
C	Artist	Melbourne
D	Engineer	Perth
E	Lawyer	Adelaide
F	Doctor	Sydney
G	Counsellor	Hobart

6. (c), D is an Engineer.
7. (a), B is the professor.
8. (d), Artist – Melbourne
9. (b), G works in Hobart
10. (d), F is the Doctor.

Question (11-16)

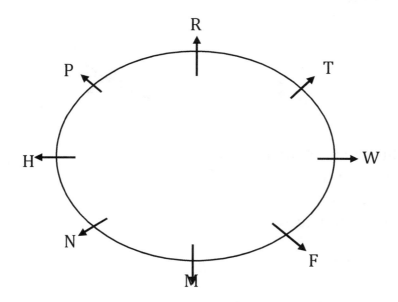

11. (a) H is immediate right of P
12. (d), N is immediate right of H
13. (d), T is immediate left of R.
14. (d), F is third to the right of H
15. (c), T is second to the right of F
16. (a), N is sitting between H and M

Question (17-20)

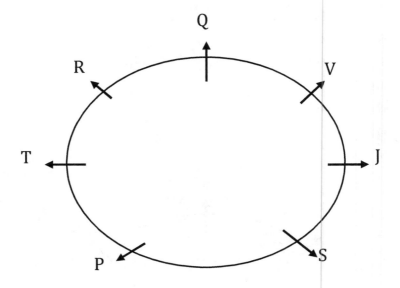

17. (b), R is the immediate right of Q
18. (c), J is second to the right of P
19. (d), 2 or 3 only
20. (a), Q is sitting between V and R.

Question (21-26)

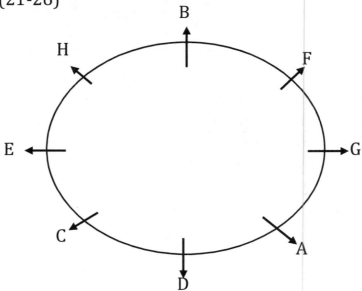

21. (b), A is between G and D
22. (c), D is 4th to the right of F is the wrong statement.
23. (b), A is between G and D
24. (d), D is immediate left of A
25. (d), None of these
26. (d), If C and G interchange their positions the A is immediate left of C.

Question (27-31)

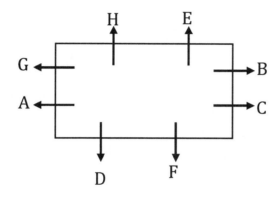

27. (d), C is sitting opposite of A
28. (b), B is next to E in clockwise direction
29. (d), Required pair = AG
30. (c), F is sitting opposite to E
31. (b), Correct Statement: E is sitting opposite to F

CPSIA information can be obtained
at www.ICGtesting.com
Printed in the USA
BVHW011328011020
590091BV00006B/236